SEEKING
A DEEPER

Walk

To James & Linda

Ephesians 3:16

H. Stuart Smith

SEEKING A DEEPER

Walk

My Search for God
A Life Long Journey

H. STUART SMITH PH.D.

TATE PUBLISHING & *Enterprises*

Published by Tate Publishing & Enterprises, LLC
127 E. Trade Center Terrace | Mustang, Oklahoma 73064 USA
1.888.361.9473 | www.tatepublishing.com

Tate Publishing is committed to excellence in the publishing industry. The company reflects the philosophy established by the founders, based on Psalm 68:11,
"The Lord gave the word and great was the company of those who published it."

Book design copyright © 2008 by Tate Publishing, LLC. All rights reserved.
Cover design by Janae J. Glass
Interior design by Kellie Southerland

Published in the United States of America

ISBN: 978-1-60604-147-5
1. Christian Living: Spiritual Growth: Discipleship and New Believer
08.05.05

This book is dedicated to my wife, Nancy. Without her encouragement, cajoling, and sometimes down-right pushing, this work would never have been completed. She has not only been my inspiration, but also my reader and best critic. She wrote the title and made many suggestions that have been incorporated in the writing.

Contents

Foreword

My wife and I live on the shores of the Chesapeake Bay. It is rewarding to awaken each morning to an expression of the bay that is different from any way this magnificent body of water has ever expressed itself before. Some mornings reveal calm waters that gently lap the sandy beach. On other mornings a northeast wind pushes the water crashing onto the land. At other times low tide reveals sand bars that are hidden when the tide is in. Foggy mornings shroud the bay with mystery. The surface of the water always reflects the color of the sky above. You cannot behold this wonder of God's creation without contemplating the God who created it.

All of mankind shares the necessity of seeking a walk with God. By this we mean living a life dedicated to Him and His teachings. The biblical letter to the Ephesians explains such a walk as living a Christian life. And, because life is in constant change, there are times when we need to seek a deeper walk with God.

A relationship with God gives us inspiration and guidance and sets moral parameters on our lives. Circumstances at different times create a range of emotions, disappointments, desires and aspirations that are personal. Our dealings with each other sometime bring us to see the need of seeking a deeper walk.

In his book, Dr. Smith begins by asking, "What is the real world?" As you read, you soon realize that he has immersed himself sufficiently in the real world to lead you through the task of facing what the real world is.

The author has done us a favor in writing *Seeking a Deeper Walk*. The book, a mixture of biography and instruction, is an inspiring account of his pilgrimage of faith. He inspires us by recounting how his faith has matured, and he instructs us by sharing his views on such subjects as "Being a Christian," "Where is God Today?" and "In the Image of God." To make the book useful for group study, he includes questions at the end of each chapter by which the reader can measure his own faith.

As the Chesapeake Bay, God's creation, is a reminder of the movements in our lives, this book is, indeed, a book for those seeking a deeper walk with God. You will be grateful for Stuart Smith's guidance in your walk.

JOHN C. DEAN
Pastor Emeritus
Larchmont Baptist Church
Norfolk, Virginia

Prologue

*"I will not die but live, and will
proclaim what the Lord has done."*
PSALM 118:17

It has taken a lifetime to write this book. I am writing it in the hope that others who find themselves on the same life-long path of uncertainty that I traveled might shorten their journey, might not have to wait so many years to reach their goal and enjoy the benefits of a strong sense of belief and commitment.

I was born on November 3, 1929, in Richmond, Virginia. The world was recovering from World War I, but the seed that would grow yet another world war had already been planted. Though most Americans were enjoying the "Roaring Twenties," the nation was actually on the brink of the "Great Depression." The economy at home became progressively worse as we moved into the 1930s. Banks collapsed, taking the life savings of millions down with them. As business after business failed, more and more Americans found themselves without jobs. In Germany, the Nazi movement was underway and in the Orient, Japan had begun to ravage its neighbors while planning its attack on the United States.

As a child growing up during those years, I was virtually unaware of all of the turmoil in the world around me. My family was less seriously affected by world affairs than most. My father was able to hold his job and we were never without food, clothing, or transportation. Though I must have been influenced in significant but subtle ways, I was not consciously aware of such things until I was about twelve years old. That's when the war began.

I remember hearing the radio announcement made by President Franklin D. Roosevelt on December 7, 1941, informing the nation that Japan had attacked us at Pearl Harbor. Within just hours we were into the war with Japan in the Pacific and with Germany and Italy in Europe.

But life went on, and we did the best we could with what we had. We lived just north of Richmond in a rural community called Glen Allen. My Saturday trips into the city to see cowboy movies ended, and my job on the nearby dairy farm went from milking cows to becoming a regular farm hand because the older boys were being called into military service. Trips to visit grandparents, who lived fifty miles away, were severely curtailed because of gasoline rationing. The little gasoline available was needed to get my father to and from work, and there weren't as many cakes and cookies due to limits on buying sugar.

It affected our play. One of the trees in our front yard became a bomber in which I flew many missions over enemy territory. Toys had to be used far beyond the point at which they would normally have been discarded.

My memories of childhood are mainly memories of good times. Even the farm work, though often hard, meant being with my friends and, I believe, we knew we were doing something useful and important. But I cannot find among those memories much to indicate that my family enjoyed any sort of meaningful relationship with God. Jesus was certainly not a regular member of our household. Prayers were pretty much limited to "Now I lay me down to sleep..." and blessings were said at meals only on special occasions. We rarely went to church and Sunday school. In Sunday school the other children always knew their memory verses. I never did. I guess that was because I didn't attend often enough to keep up with the lessons. I do remember Reverend Carner. What I remember most is that he cried when he preached. I thought that was strange. It seemed especially strange because I had no feeling that the things he talked about were important enough to cry over. I didn't understand.

World War II and adolescence hit me at about the same time. Adolescence had the greater impact on me, by far. Though the war appeared to go on forever, I don't remember that it affected me much beyond the cutbacks in gasoline and sugar and my job on the farm. We cheered when we saw pictures of our troops in the newsreels but actual news coverage was scarce compared to today's "on-the-spot" television coverage of events as they happen. I suspect that I hadn't lived long enough to be truly aware of the changes brought on by the war.

Adolescence was quite another matter. Suddenly, I was no longer a child. I had a new mind and a new body. I could do things I had never done before. I had feelings I had never had before. I remember that as a young child, life was always in the here and now. I had no sense of the future when I was eight years old. It seemed as if things would always be the same. That notion neither distressed nor pleased me. It's just the way it was. But along with adolescence came thoughts of tomorrow and the next year, and on into the future. There was a feeling of life opening up much like a bud becomes a flower.

In those days life for teenagers was much different from what it is today. A whole generation of young men was away at war. Those who were too young to serve in the military had to step up to fill the gaps. It meant we had real jobs with real responsibilities. Adolescents were accepted for what they could do, not their age. When I was thirteen I entered high school. At fourteen I had a driver's license and worked after school as a farm hand and a grocery clerk. I played semi-pro baseball with men who were too old to be drafted by the military. We grew up rapidly because we had to.

High school was a great period in my life. I was active in sports, started and edited the student newspaper, served in the student government, and actually enjoyed going to school. We had none of the pressures faced by today's youngsters. Drugs, sex, alcohol, and automobiles were not part of our lives. We dated, but sex was out of the question. And because of the war, no one had use of an automobile for anything other than necessities. We had permits to drive, but no cars. But we had a good time.

Life for me during those years was wonderful. It was the kind of life we wish every child could have. It was safe, filled with opportunities, and free from many of the pressures that can be so traumatic for today's children.

And finally the war was over. Veterans of military service returned home, some to high schools, but more to college, thanks to the benefits of the GI Bill. New cars, gasoline, and sugar were again available. Times were good. Perhaps for me they were too good. God had been only a small part of my early childhood. In adolescence, He was not there at all, so far as I could tell. I have absolutely no memory of even going to church except to attend my cousin's wedding at a military chapel and my grandparents' funerals during those years. There was no feeling of a personal relationship with God—none at all. I didn't believe or disbelieve. I just didn't think about it.

Things changed drastically after high school. I became the first member of my family to go to college. It had been planned for some time that I would go to the University of Richmond. Living at home, using some money left by my grandparents, and part-time work would see me through. However, at virtually the last minute, those plans were changed. One of my high school football coaches accepted a job at Hampden-Sydney College, a small Presbyterian school, and he urged me to come to school there to play football. My scholarship consisted of one-half of my school fees and a part-time job at the campus post office. For the first time in my life I was living away from home. Except for my coach, there wasn't a soul at the school I had ever met before my arrival there.

I plunged in—studying hard, playing football, and joining a fraternity. The fraternity house was my home away from home. One of the older students, a veteran of military service, took me under his wing. He taught me to shoot pool in the basement of the fraternity house, but mainly we just spent time being friends.

I attended chapel services regularly because it was required, as was a course in the New Testament. I became friends with several students who were going into the ministry. But God was still not real to me. However, through the chapel services, the courses, and my friends, I was being confronted. I could not avoid God's presence even though I was not taking advantage of the opportunities available to me.

Playing football was no longer the fun it had been in high school. We won only one game that year, and when the season was over I decided that I didn't want to play any more football. That meant I could not return to Hampden-Sydney. The cost was more than my family could handle.

The following year I enrolled at the University of Richmond but lived at home. The shift from total immersion in the life at Hampden-Sydney to going to classes but little else at the University of Richmond was something of a step back in time for me. All of my social life was off-campus, back with the crowd I had run around with as a teenager. I even spent my free afternoons coaching the junior varsity football team at my old high school. My year at Hampden-Sydney faded into the past. Nevertheless, I have always felt that that one year was a most important one for me. The experiences made an impression that I was not aware of until years later.

For the next two years, I applied myself to an accelerated program at school, worked part-time in a grocery store, coached my teams at the high school, and dated. At the end of the summer of 1950 I graduated from college, got married, and accepted a job as teacher and coach at the high school I had attended and where I was already coaching.

I was stepping into the adult world. Everything seemed to be going well. One other significant experience was on the horizon, an experience that has been with me now for over fifty years.

Preparation for marriage included meeting with the Presbyterian minister who was to perform the ceremony. In addition to attending services in his church, we met several times to talk on a personal level about God's place in our lives. It was not the content of these meetings that turned out to be important. In fact, though I was intellectually aware of the content of our discussions, I never allowed it to bring me to grips with the real issues in my life at that time and how those might affect a decision to marry. But that is another story. The immediate impact of those meetings was the association with the young minister. He was a quiet, soft-spoken man who seemed to me to represent the Christian ideal. I cannot say just why that happened. If I were to meet him today, I suspect my impressions would be positive but quite different. But because of his witness, through his life more than his words, I began to feel a personal bond with Jesus Christ.

With this minister's encouragement, I started to attend church regularly. I got involved in the activities of the church and Sunday school, especially those involving the young adults. There were social activities and retreats along with the regular program. I played softball on the church team and represented our young adults at conferences.

In the meantime, I was beginning a career as a teacher and coach. My assignment that first year included teaching a bright and energetic group of eighth-grade youngsters and courses in French and English. Afternoons were taken up with coaching the junior varsity football team.

At this point in my life I experienced what I felt was a powerful calling to the ministry. This calling came as a spoken message, which I believed was God speaking directly and clearly to me and telling me that He wanted me in full-time Christian service. When I spoke about this to my minister friend, he suggested I talk with staff members at the Presbyterian seminary in Richmond. They suggested that perhaps I was hallucinating and should not act too hastily. After being confronted with all of the "logical" reasons I should not undertake seminary studies at that time, I rejected the calling.

Shortly after this experience, I was called to military service in the Navy where I served as a junior naval officer during the Korean conflict. Though this military experience exposed me to lifestyles and values that I had not previously known existed, the military life was not for me and I left the Navy after four years of service. However, it was during this period of military service that I had the opportunity to help with the establishment of a new church in the neighborhood where I had lived. This proved to be a very rewarding experience, but again, I failed to realize the real source of the richness of that work and it soon faded into the past.

The military phase of my life was followed by a very short career in the life insurance business and five years as employment manager for a large corporation in Richmond, Virginia. During this period my family grew to include three children. The family attended church, probably because it seemed to be the right thing to do. Spiritually, I was at a low ebb except for a brief period of involvement in prayer groups that were established in the Richmond area in conjunction with a Billy Graham Crusade. These groups proved to be dynamic, and, for a time, I was on another spiritual high. But the career in business, which at first seemed so exciting and challenging, became increasingly empty and meaningless. The soul searching at this period in my life led me to make a major vocational decision that was soon followed by the opening up of an opportunity I never imagined would be available to me. I was invited by Virginia Polytechnic Institute and State University to join the staff of their Cooperative Work-Study Program. During the five years spent there I earned a master's degree in vocational education. The highlights of those years included raising three great children, my work, coaching a Little League baseball team, and making some wonderful friends. My involvement with church was fairly regular, but continued to be casual.

In the spring of 1965, after completing my master's degree, I vowed never to go to school again. However, by mid-summer I found myself planning to enroll at the University of Virginia to study for a Ph.D. in educational psychology and human development. The two years at the university were difficult and challenging but, at the same time, very rewarding. I earned my degree, taught courses for the university, and worked in the Research Center doing educational research. In 1967, I accepted a position at Virginia Commonwealth University in Richmond as director of the Child Study Center and assistant professor of education and psychology.

My church affiliation continued as in the past, attending more or less regularly but with no real commitment or enthusiasm. I became a deacon and an elder in the Presbyterian Church, but somehow never became truly involved. In addition, problems both at work and in my family life led to yet another move, another change of jobs.

In 1971, I accepted a teaching position as professor of psychology with Tidewater Community College which was just establishing a new campus in Virginia Beach. The years there were very fulfilling and meaningful to me professionally. Being part of an institution from the day it first opened with about eight hundred students to one with over thirteen thousand students was a challenge, to say the least.

My personal life proved to be less successful. In 1983 my marriage of thirty-three years ended in divorce. Though I was active in a Baptist church and ordained as a deacon there, my spiritual life was still of no great importance to me. Following the divorce, I separated myself from virtually all contact with any church and immersed myself in my teaching and in caring for my mother and her sister who came to live with me.

Finally, in 1985, I met Nancy, the person whose friendship and, later, love and devotion would turn my lonely and unhappy life around. We were married in December of 1986. With her support and encouragement, I renewed my interest in church, though still on a rather casual basis. Then, in the summer of 1991, we went to a gospel sing convention. We had planned to stop in for a short time, but found ourselves staying for the full two-day program. We met a number of the singers, some of whom have become friends. I found them to be sincere, honest, good folks whose lives reflected the message they brought in song. Through them, and through Nancy, I came to the exciting realization of what it truly meant to have God at the center of my life. The Scriptures came alive in a way I had never experienced before, and becoming involved with a body of believers became a compelling necessity.

Then, wouldn't you know it? Satan showed up in a big way. That's what he always does. Just as we draw closer to God, as we develop a truly personal relationship with Jesus, Satan will try to interfere. He will do everything he can to cause you to question your God. In our case he struck with full force in the areas of finances and health.

Financially, we lost virtually all of our savings, which had been invested in real estate, and we experienced a severe loss of income due to economic conditions and health problems. Nancy developed Guillain-Barre Syndrome on January 25, 1992, a condition that paralyzed her from the waist down. Finally, more than a year and a half later, she was able to return to work. In July of 1992, I suffered a severe heart attack followed five months later by heart by-pass surgery. Two months after that I had another heart attack and the by-pass surgery had to be repeated. Satan used these unfortunate experiences to try to plant doubt in our minds, doubt that God really loved us and was in control of our circumstances.

This may all sound dreadful, and in some ways I guess it was. However, Nancy and I judge this year to have been a blessing. It brought us even closer together and it has strengthened ties with friends and family. It has given us a chance to witness by sharing with others what God's strength, healing, and presence have meant to us. People have marveled at our good spirit and positive outlook during those difficult times.

I had begun some preliminary work on this book when I had the heart attack in July of 1992. As I mentioned, it was a very serious attack. My doctors did not expect me to survive and repeatedly prepared

Nancy for the worst. But I did survive and through it all, I was reminded of Psalm 118:17:

"I will not die but live, and will proclaim what the Lord has done."

This verse was brought to me by both my daughter and a minister friend while I was still in the hospital and quite ill. The message seems clear. God has not released me from that calling issued many years ago. He has work for me to do and I believe very strongly that at least one of the things to which I am called is to share my Christian walk with you through writing this book.

The past fifteen years have been wonderful. Nancy and I continue to grow closer and to share our golden years as graciously and thankfully as possible. We had a wonderful church experience for several years at Suburban Christian Church, then after moving we began attending and fell in love with St. John's Baptist Church. We established and taught a Sunday school class for several years, I headed the Baptist Men's group for two years, and we have made many great friends. The book has been on the back burner, but I think this is a matter of God's timing. Throughout most of the years of my life, and certainly during this past fifteen years, I have wrestled with many questions. The path to becoming a Christian in more than name only has included a number of issues, some of which have been difficult to resolve. And I expect and hope there will be more. I want to continue to grow.

It is my hope that by sharing my experiences and my answers to these questions with you, and letting you know what God has meant to me, I might touch a chord in you that I had always wanted so desperately to have touched in me.

What I write is what I believe. I do not ask that you agree with me, but I do hope and pray that by sharing my life and beliefs with you, you will be challenged in a way that will deepen and enrich your own beliefs, your spiritual life, and your walk with God.

Introduction

*"… He causes his sun to rise on the evil and the good,
and sends rain on the righteous and the unrighteous."*
MATTHEW 5:45

What is the real world?

Is it only the world of nature, a world that operates on its own power without help or intervention from any outside sources? The Naturalists tell us it is that way. In their view, nature is everything. There is nothing else. And nature is orderly. It runs according to principles that can be learned and understood by rigorously pursuing the ways of science. Included in this natural view of things is the idea that every event has a cause and that cause had a cause, etc. Suppose it rains. Why does it rain? If we can answer that question we may next ask what caused the conditions that caused it to rain. And we can keep on asking these questions until we arrive at the beginning. At that point science just throws up its hands and says, "I don't know what, if anything, came before the beginning."

Or is the real world a supernatural place? Is there a God who moment-by-moment decides on and controls every event that happens? Does it rain because God decided today that in some particular place it would rain a certain amount and it wouldn't rain in other places? Does God decide if today is the day for your car battery to go bad, or for Aunt Susie to develop cancer, or for you to get a raise? If we believe God is manipulating every event that happens as it happens, then we could just throw science away. It would be a complete waste of time to try to study forces that have no real pattern other than that they reflect what God wishes to do today. And the answer to what causes things to happen would always be that God wanted it that way today.

There is a third view of the real world, the view that I hold and the one on which this book is based. It is my belief that God created nature and the laws that govern it. He made this creation good and, therefore, does not need to tinker with it constantly. This nature can be studied by science and from these studies we can learn much that is useful about our world. But I also believe that God is still with us.

He did not abandon His creation after making it. And when it is necessary for His purposes, He can enter into events and arrange them accordingly. For example, when men die they do not come back to life on this earth. But there have been instances, most notably Jesus, when resurrection did occur. But it was necessary for God's purposes for that to happen. The same can be said for all of the Scriptural references to resurrection. In a more here and now example, I know that God saw to it that I recovered from a serious heart attack against all of the expectations of medical science, because there was still work for me to do.

Having this view allows us to believe in miracles. Naturalists cannot accept miracles because in their view miracles simply cannot happen. Those who believe that God is manipulating every event cannot believe in miracles because in their view everything is a miracle. But I believe in miracles and everything I have to say in this book is based on that view of the world.

When God created everything, the universe, earth and everything found there, including man, He placed man in the Garden of Eden. The Garden of Eden was a world free of danger and sorrow, free even from death. It was a world of abundance, a perfect place, heaven on earth. But, as we all know, things didn't work out too well for the occupants of the garden, Adam and Eve.

After living in the Garden of Eden for a time,

Adam and Eve were confronted with a choice. They were tempted to do what God had told them not to do; to eat from the tree of the knowledge of good and evil. They were helped in this matter by Satan, represented as a serpent in the story. It was the serpent who suggested that it would be all right to eat the forbidden fruit:

> Now the serpent was more crafty than any of the wild animals the Lord God had made. He said to the woman, "Did God really say, You must not eat from any tree in the Garden?" The woman said to the serpent, "We may eat fruit from the trees in the Garden, but God did say, You must not eat fruit from the tree that is in the middle of the garden, and you must not touch it, or you will die. You will not surely die," the serpent said to the woman. "For God knows that when you eat of it your eyes will be opened, and you will be like God, knowing good and evil."
>
> GENESIS 3:1–5

This is the first record we have of Satan trying to come between us and God. And this time he succeeded. Adam and Eve ate from the forbidden tree. As a result, God removed them from the garden and placed them in the world of nature; a world of danger and sorrow, the real world we live in today.

The real world is the beauty of a spring day but

also the destruction of a hurricane. It is the glory of the heavens on a starlit night and the eruption of a volcano. It is the joy of a newborn baby and the unspeakable grief experienced with the death of a child. It is financial success and economic ruin. It is political freedom and unbearable oppression. It is the height of ecstasy and the depths of despair. Christians, like all other residents of earth, must deal with all of these things. We may experience joy and happiness, but we must remember that we are not immune from the tragedies this world sometimes sends our way.

Adam and Eve made the choice to disobey God and, as a result, everything changed:

> And the Lord God said, "The man has now become like one of us, knowing good and evil. He must not be allowed to reach out his hand and take also from the tree of life and eat, and live forever." So the Lord God banished him from the Garden of Eden to work the ground from which he had been taken.
>
> GENESIS 3:22–24

Certainly Adam and Eve were not immune to conditions in the world outside of Eden. We learn from Chapter 3 of the book of Genesis that when they arrived in the new world:

1. They knew they were naked.

2. They became afraid.

3. God increased woman's pain in childbirth.

4. God cursed the ground from which Adam would toil to grow food.

5. The ground produced thorns and thistles.

6. Man would sweat to grow his food.

7. Man would die.

Now it really doesn't matter whether you choose to believe this story of the relationship between God and man as a literally true, historical account of what happened to a man named Adam and a woman named Eve in a place called the Garden of Eden, or as an allegorical account describing mankind's slipping away from a condition of oneness with God. Either way, the lesson is the same. And it is the lesson that is important, the message that God is attempting to give us. If we insist on waiting for scientific confirmation of every story in the Bible before accepting it, we will miss the lesson completely.

From the day that man chose to live outside of God's realm he began to live in the real world where he knew guilt and shame, felt fear and pain, toiled among the thorns and thistles to earn his bread, and none of his accomplishments would come easily. He would sweat for his successes. He would die. And God has never promised to release us from the laws of nature. Christians get sick when their bodies are attacked by germs. They are injured and killed when they fall or when they are struck by large moving objects or by bullets and knives. This is the world we will live in until the coming of the new heaven and the new earth.

But why should it be that way? Why did God leave us vulnerable to nature? Why are those who love him not protected? Can't we go back to the Garden of Eden?

The answer to the question about the Garden of Eden is yes. We could go back to the Garden of Eden if God wanted it that way. Actually, He could have arranged things so that we never left the Garden in the first place. God could have seen to it that Adam and Eve did not eat from the forbidden tree. After all, these were His own creations and He could have created them in any form and with any characteristics He wished them to have. He could have created them, and us, to be like puppets with no will of our own. He could have made Adam and Eve totally obedient to Him with no capacity to dis-obey or turn away. He could have chosen to control our every move and every thought. If He had done that, Adam and Eve would still be there, living for-ever in that perfect place.

The Garden of Eden sounds a little bit like heaven, doesn't it? There was no death, and I think it is reasonable for us to assume, no illness or pain, no unfulfilled needs, no troubles or sorrows. Wouldn't that be a wonderful life? It may seem that way to us, especially when life appears to be full of burdens. We are all very aware of the presence of danger in our lives and the lives of those close to us. Many of us are coping with daily conflicts. Don't all of us yearn, at times, for perfect serenity, the kind that Adam and Eve could have had if only they had cho-sen to obey God?

But for some reason, His reason, God didn't want it that way. From the moment of Adam and Eve's creation they had the capacity to make choices, and that included the choice of disobedience along with many other bad choices we humans might make. When we realize that God called His creation good even though He had given man this awesome ability to make choices, even the choice to turn away from Him, and the responsibility that goes with that, we have to conclude that that is the way He wanted it to be. Man's ability to make choices, including dis-obeying or rejecting God, was part of the plan from the beginning. And God called it good.

So here we are, in the real world, a world that is beautiful and abundant, but also a world of danger.

Why would God want it this way? Why not bring

His children into a Garden of Eden world and simply leave us there to live in blissful peace and happiness? Have you, as a parent, ever wished you could do that for your children? Wouldn't it be an ideal world if our children could be raised in complete safety and perfect health, a world with no dangers, a world in which everyone is happy and free from troubles? Or would it? Apparently God doesn't think so. Though we can never truly know why God does things, we can try to understand to the extent of our limited human ability to know Him.

God gave us a world full of joys, love, happiness, and an abundance of blessings. He also gave us a world of pain, anger, hatred, danger, and sadness. And when He put us into this world He gave us the ability to choose the attitudes we would hold, the paths we would take, the friends with whom we would associate, and what we would believe. Instead of making us happy robots, He gave us the power to choose and to be responsible for our choices. We are subjected to the good and the bad and are allowed to decide how we will react. And most importantly, He allows us to choose Him or turn away from Him.

The relationship we have with God is so powerfully portrayed in the story of the Prodigal Son. Here we have the story of a young man who chose to leave his family home, his father and his brother, and strike out on his own. We know the dismal result of his decision, but we also know the joy that was felt when he reunited with his father. Remember, too, the older brother. He remained at home and enjoyed all of the benefits of his family's wealth and status. And yet, when his brother returned, he resented the enthusiasm with which his return was welcomed by the father.

This story should not be understood to mean that we should all be Prodigal Sons. Those who stay at home with the father, as the older brother did in this story, enjoy the benefits of that relationship all of the time. He did not have to leave home in order for his father to love him and lavish him with all of the blessings he had to give. What we must learn is that when everything is always there for us, so easy to obtain, we can lose sight of the source. We cease to appreciate what we have and where it is coming from. I believe that God, much like us, wants to be appreciated by His children. Perhaps Adam and Eve, like the Prodigal's older brother, had it too easy in the Garden of Eden. Perhaps they forgot where all of their blessings were coming from. While we are in this human form we probably need to experience a certain amount of the negative side of the real world in order to appreciate the blessings that we have and the source of those blessings. And so God, who is a much wiser parent than we could ever be, has given us a world in which we can see and feel Him in both joy and tragedy.

If we were robots living in a perfect world we would have no capacity to revere and honor God. It seems to me that God must have put us in this kind of world with the ability to choose from both the good and the bad because without that ability we would not be able to worship Him. If our responses to God were automatic, reflex reactions, we would be responding but not worshipping. Imagine having a robot that opened your front door when you came home and greeted you each time with:

All praise to you , Master. Bless your name . . . .click

Every time you enter you hear the same automatic greeting. Not much honor there, is there? Only if the one greeting us has a choice to either greet us or ignore us does the greeting really matter. Don't you suppose God is pleased when we honor Him because we choose to?

There are many mysteries in the Bible. But this is abundantly clear; God loves us and He wants us to know, love, and worship Him. He wants this so desperately that He sent his Son to reveal the Father to us and show us the way home. Even the Son, Himself, had to suffer in order for us to understand and give ourselves back to Him. But we still must choose.

We can choose to live as if God did not exist at all. We can remain totally in the world of nature. But God also allows us the choice of knowing Him, of having Him at the center of our lives, of feeling that peace that comes with oneness with Him and of knowing His mercy, grace, and salvation.

Christians live in the real world and are subject

to both its pleasures and its pain. But we march through it all to a higher calling than anything the real world can offer. We are in the world but not of the world. We have chosen to keep God at the center of our lives, to depend on Him and to thank Him for the very gift of life and all that life brings to us. And He, in turn, promises to be with us, to lead us on the journey. That is the promise to those who love God. As we march through this world, we do it with God at our side and Christ as our guide through all of the dangers and tragedies, as well as the joys and happiness.

And He has shown us how, when this life on earth is done, we can return to Eden, to heaven, and live with Him there forever.

Some Questions for Thought and Discussion

1. With which view of the world are you most comfortable?

2. How does your view of miracles compare with the author's view?

3. Why do you think God gave us the ability to make choices?

4. Can Christians count on God to protect them from dangers and diseases?

5. Do you believe that we need to experience

some of the negative side of the real world in order to appreciate the good?

CHAPTER 1

In the Image of God

"What is man that you are mindful of him,
the son of man that you care for him?
You made him a little lower than the heavenly
beings and crowned him with glory and honor."
PSALM 8:4–5

As a Christian, I find myself thinking about my relationship to God. I am thinking here of my kinship. In what way am I created in God's image? What traits do we share in common? What is the connecting link between God and me?

We live in the real world, the world that God made and called good. We are part of that world. In fact, we hold a very special place in God's creation.

So God created man in his own image, in
the image of God he created him; male and
female he created them. God blessed them
and said to them, "Be fruitful and increase
in number; fill the earth and subdue it. Rule
over the fish of the sea and the birds of the
air and over every living creature that moves
on the ground."

GENESIS 1:27–28

But who are we? Who is this person that God has
made and put in charge of His world?

I taught college courses in psychology and human
development for more than thirty years. These were
courses that are supposed to help us understand ourselves. We learn about many of our characteristics—
how we learn, think, and behave. However, many
times students would remark at the end of a course
that what we had studied was all very interesting,
but something important had been left out. We had
not examined man's spiritual qualities.

Of course, the students were right. Psychology
does not deal with spirituality except in a very superficial way. It may tabulate what proportion of the
population goes to church, or it may survey opinions regarding religious issues. But the limitations of
science make it impossible for scientific fields such
as psychology to ever fully understand and explain
man. Psychology can only deal with the natural
world, the world that can be explained by scientifi-

cally studying the laws of nature that apply to man and his behavior. But science cannot study those qualities that fall outside of the natural part of man. Our spiritual qualities are not natural and, therefore, are not matters with which science can deal.

The fact that psychology does not study man's spiritual qualities does not mean that the field is anti-religious or dangerous, as some would have us believe. It simply means that psychology only studies man's natural qualities, those qualities that are part of and which do react to the laws which govern nature. That is a large part of what we are and what we will be until Christ comes again. And it is that part—the natural part—that science and psychology can study.

But there is so much more to us than just those natural parts that can be studied scientifically. When scientists tell us that a certain percentage of us react in a certain way, or heal in a certain way, and another percentage respond differently to what seem to be the same circumstances, we may want an explanation for the differences. If we keep asking the why questions, we eventually are told that science cannot answer, things are just "that way." Science said I would die when I had a heart attack and that the woman in the unit next to me would live. She died and I lived. Why? We don't really know except to say that there is something about us that science doesn't understand and cannot know because it isn't "natural." It is "supernatural" and, as a result, cannot be known by science, which is limited to the natural world.

I've wandered off the track a bit. But there is a point to this. If we are going to understand that wonderful being we call man, perhaps we would do well to consider knowledge from many sources, science included. There is only one reservation for Christians. Scientific knowledge must not contradict Scripture. As Christians, we hold the Word of God to be the final authority.

Christians who have been troubled by the apparent conflict between science and the Bible should read *The Science of God* by Gerald L. Schroeder and *The Language of God* by Francis S. Collins. These eminent Christian scientists show us that science and the Bible are not in conflict. On the contrary, they converge and complement one another.

Let's go back to the original question.

Who is this person God has made and put in charge of his creation? What makes us human and, at the same time, in the image of God?

These questions would be easy to answer if Scripture dealt with them in a direct and simple way. However, I can't find a simple answer in the Bible. This doesn't mean that the Bible has nothing to say. Far from it. It says so much that it is difficult to get down to basics. But let's try.

I believe the Bible teaches us that we consist of three basic parts: body, soul, and spirit. Every person possesses all three of these characteristics from the moment of conception. But the way these parts work together may differ widely from person to person. A biblical source in which these three terms are used to describe man is found in Paul's first letter to the Thessalonians.

Paul writes:

> May God himself, the God of peace, sanctify you through and through. May your whole spirit, soul and body be kept blameless at the coming of our Lord Jesus Christ.
>
> 1 THESSALONIANS 5:23

In describing the complete person, Paul uses three terms; body, soul, and spirit. To what do these terms refer and how do these parts interact?

THE BODY

The body is a gift from God. It is the vessel in which we live while we are on this earth. Though made perfect in the beginning in Adam and Eve, the body became imperfect and fragile, subject to pain, and doomed to die. It is the body in which Jesus lived and was crucified, died, and was buried.

This body belongs to the real world and is subject to all of the laws that govern the real world. These are the laws that can become the basis for such fields as medicine, biology, psychology, and biochemistry.

If the natural body is affected by viruses or bacteria, it will become ill. It is made of cells that eventually wear out, and it is subject to stresses that can speed up the wearing out process. If it is struck hard enough, it will break. Feed it contaminated food and it will be poisoned. No one is excused from these laws.

The body is also the source of many wonders, gifts from God. For example, the body has a great capacity for healing. If you cut yourself, the cut will heal. Bruise yourself and it will eventually clear up and fade away. Develop an ear infection and your white blood cells go to work immediately to rid you of the intruders. Foreign bodies that find their way under your skin are rejected. Even pain, which we would all like to avoid, serves a valuable purpose by signaling to us that something is wrong.

The body has an immune system that protects us from all sorts of problems. We possess the means to reproduce, creating more bodies in ways we are slowly beginning to understand. We have a nervous system that allows us to experience pleasure, feel pain, sense and respond to the world around us, and to keep all of the systems of the body working, and working in harmony. We can feel good and we can feel bad. We enjoy good food, the touch of a loved one, and sexual pleasures. Nature provides all of this, the good and the bad, and because it is part of nature, science may someday lead us to a full understanding of the body's structures and functions.

The bodies of Christians, Jews, Hindus, and atheists are all the same. They are all created according to the same natural laws and they all grow and develop according to those natural laws. One's religious beliefs do not change that. Our bodies are part of the real world.

THE SOUL

The soul, in its most basic form, comes directly from the natural body. It is the expression in thoughts, feelings, attitudes, and beliefs of the activity of the brain. The soul is the source of our emotions and our will. It is closely related to our motives, our drives, and the goals toward which we direct our energies. The soul, in its natural condition, is what the ancient Greeks referred to as "Psyche." It is the mechanism that allows us to go beyond mere reflex or conditioned behavior to creating or making choices. It also happens to be the point of entry for both Satan and the Holy Spirit and, in that case, becomes a battleground for these forces. But more on that later.

In its natural condition, the condition that has existed since the fall of Adam and Eve, the soul has been focused on the natural body and the natural world, the real world. In this condition, the soul is concerned with self-gratification, achievement of material goals, and all sorts of matters of a worldly nature. It is both in and of the world. Under these circumstances our backs are turned on God, so to speak. This is the man described in Galatians 4:19–21 whose behavior is characterized by Paul as including sexual immorality, impurity and debauchery, idolatry and witchcraft, hatred, discord, jealousy, fits of rage, selfish ambition, dissensions, factions and envy, drunkenness, orgies, and the like.

Had Paul been reading our daily newspapers or watching television? What he has described in Galatians sounds like the picture of modern man. Just recently a report came over the news concerning rioting and looting in a city whose team had just won a national sports championship. Celebrating in these modern times seems to include arson, looting, shootings, and vandalism. Those celebrating trashed their own city. And it happens over and over again. What is even more distressing is the tendency to condone such behaviors in many instances. If it's "the in thing to do" or if "everybody is doing it," then it is supposedly all right, at least according to many sources which do influence thought and behavior in the world.

For so long as it is operating in the realm of nature, the real world, the soul will function pretty much in accord with the way Paul described it, conditions that are verified by numerous studies done in the field of psychology. However, it doesn't take long to discover that people don't always react according to these principles. There is yet another piece to the puzzle which we must examine.

THE SPIRIT

We are body, soul, and also spirit.

> Then God said, "Let us make man in our image, in our likeness, and let them rule over

the fish of the sea and the birds of the air, over the livestock, over all the earth, and over all the creatures that move along the ground." So God created man in his own image, in the image of God he created him; male and female he created them.

GENESIS 1:26–27

I believe that when the Bible tells us that we are created in the image of God, it is telling us that we are blessed from the beginning with the presence of God, who is spirit within us. This is not the Holy Spirit who comes only when we seek Him, ask for Him, and open ourselves to receive Him. The spirit that comes to all of us through the act of creation is that special quality which makes us children of God, made in His image. It is what raises you above the other parts of creation. It is what establishes our kinship with the Father.

Paul makes this point about God being within us from the beginning in the first chapter of Romans. Quoting from the Living Bible because of its somewhat greater clarity on this point:

But God shows his anger from heaven against all sinful, evil men who push away the truth from them. For the truth about God is known to them instinctively.

ROMANS 1:18–19, LB

A very crude comparison can be made between this spirit which links us with our Heavenly Father and the genetic tie we have with our biological parents. Through the genes we share some of the qualities of our parents but we are not identical to them. Though the genes are the basis for our kinship, they do not insure that we will love our parents or hold them at the center of our lives. We can, in fact, reject our parents. And yet, at a deep, deep level of our being we are still aware of the original bond. How often do people who are separated at an early age from their parents still want to make some kind of connection with them? It may be only curiosity, but the yearning is still there.

Similarly, but in a much more profound way, we are aware of our kinship with God. In every culture, from the most civilized to the most primitive, we find some sort of religion, some indication of the sense of oneness with a Supreme Being. Do you know someone who professes no personal bond with God but who claims, at times, to sense the presence of God, perhaps in a beautiful sunset:? And why are so many Bibles sold, even to people who never read them? Could it be that there is a flickering spirit deep within that urges us to identify, in some way, with God?

This quality which makes all mankind continuously aware of the existence of God and our kinship with Him is what Paul refers to as spirit. While we are living here on Earth our spirit resides within us.

When we are saved through God's grace and mercy our spirit is assured of spending eternity with God. If we are not saved, our spirit spends eternity apart from God, in hell.

The spirit is not of the world. It is temporarily in the world while we are here in our earthly bodies, but it has no earthly connections. It is God in us.

BODY-SOUL-SPIRIT CONNECTION

Thus, we have a body which is totally in the real world, the world of nature, and we have the spirit, which is not of the real world at all. Between these two lies the soul. The soul is partially in the real world but it is sensitive to, and affected by, the spirit and things of the spiritual world. It is through the soul that the spiritual forces may influence the body.

In our natural state, the natural parts of the system work closely together in accordance with natural laws. That is, the body and the soul interact continuously with only a trace of influence from the spirit. In order to become a complete person, a person in whom all three elements of body, soul, and spirit are dynamically interacting with one another, we must introduce yet another element, the Holy Spirit.

THE HOLY SPIRIT

The key to enjoying the fulfillment of God's promises in our lives and becoming a whole person is the acceptance of the Holy Spirit. There really is no

other way. Read the words of Jesus as He spoke to
Nicodemus about being born again:

> Jesus answered, "I tell you the truth, no
> one can enter the kingdom of God unless
> he is born of water and the Spirit. Flesh
> gives birth to flesh, but the Spirit gives
> birth to spirit."
>
> JOHN 3:5–6

Notice that the word *spirit* is sometimes spelled
with a capital letter and sometimes not. The capi-
talized word refers to the Holy Spirit, a part of the
God-head, and the non-capitalized form refers to
the spirit within us.

Just before Jesus was crucified, He promised
to send the Counselor, the Holy Spirit, to His
followers:

> "If you love me, you will obey what I
> command. And I will ask the Father, and He
> will give you another Counselor to be with
> you forever-the Spirit of truth. The world
> cannot accept him, because it neither sees
> him nor knows him. But you know him, for
> he lives with you and will be in you."
>
> JOHN 14:15–17

In this passage Jesus refers to "another Counselor,"
one to replace Him in the daily lives of His followers.

In an appearance to His apostles after His crucifixion and resurrection, Jesus again spoke of the Holy Spirit;

> On one occasion, while He was eating with them, He gave them this command: "Do not leave Jerusalem, but wait for the gift my Father promised, which you have heard me speak about. For John baptized with water, but in a few days you will be baptized with the Holy Spirit."
>
> ACTS 1:4–5

Christians are familiar with what followed. On the day of Pentecost the followers of Jesus experienced what we call the Baptism of the Holy Spirit, an event that transformed this band of confused, uncertain, and maybe even frightened individuals into a powerful force that changed the world forever.

I must confess that this matter of the Holy Spirit has been a very confusing part of my own Christian experience. I cannot recall that much emphasis was placed on the significance and role of the Holy Spirit in the life of the individual in the churches I attended in my early years as a Christian. It's not that the Holy Spirit was totally ignored. I learned about the Triune God—God the Father, God the Son, and God the Holy Spirit. I learned that when adults are baptized in the Methodist Church, we used the phrase, "May they be filled with the Holy

Spirit..." and when we repeat the Apostles' Creed we would say, "I believe in the Holy Spirit..."

In spite of the many references to the Holy Spirit, it just didn't make much of an impression on me. In fact, I had an image that "Holy Ghost" people rolled around on the floor, used snakes in their worship services, and were so zealous in their religion that they were a nuisance to anyone coming into contact with them. Churches either gave only lip service to the Holy Spirit or it became an all-consuming feature of their spiritual life, or so it seemed to me.

I tended to fall into that large group of Christians who tried very hard to keep their Christianity under control. I didn't want to be different if being different might result in being rejected or seeming to be strange to the people I interacted with on a daily basis. It was okay to be a Baptist, or a Methodist, or a Presbyterian, but being a Christian was something else again.

I was comfortable with Christianity as a "way of life." It seemed to me that the values taught—love God and your fellow man—were great standards to live by. But I was reluctant to "Let go and let God." I didn't want to let my Christianity make me different. I fit the description found in Revelation:

"I know your deeds, that you are neither cold nor hot. I wish you were either one or the other!" Revelation 3:15

But the following verse was even more troubling:

"So, because you are lukewarm-neither hot nor cold-I am about to spit you out of my mouth." Revelation 3:16

My reluctance to accept the Holy Spirit and turn my life over to God was a clear indication of a lack of faith. I trusted God to save me, but I didn't trust Him enough to give Him control of my life. When it came to issues like finances, personal relationships, or vocational plans, I remained firmly rooted in the natural world. I would pray about such matters, but my prayers were usually asking God to do what I wanted to do instead of praying for His will to be done. I was in control, or thought I was. Is it surprising that I experienced very little feeling that God was truly a personal God?

My attempts to avoid the Holy Spirit went on for many years. Somehow I was able to overlook the teachings in the New Testament regarding the Holy Spirit. When I would read books or hear sermons and testimonials on the subject, I managed to reject what I heard or read as being exaggerations or wishful thinking. I put those who made claims about the role of the Holy Spirit in their lives into the category of desperate souls clinging to a myth in an effort to give some meaning to their otherwise meaningless lives. Their claims just didn't "make sense."

You know what happened. Had things remained as they were, I wouldn't have written this book. After so many years of knowing there had to be more to being a Christian than I was experiencing, something happened that changed everything. I stopped resisting. I stopped fighting. I asked the Holy Spirit to come into my life. I no longer wanted God just to be on call, but wanted Him to be with me every day, in everything that went on in my life. I didn't want Him to do everything for me, but to be there with me and, when necessary, to guide me. I used that ability that God has given us all, the ability to choose. And I chose the Holy Spirit.

I chose to invite the Holy Spirit into my life and at that point some wonderful things began to happen. I became a new person.

SOME QUESTIONS FOR THOUGHT AND DISCUSSION

1. Has it been your experience that education has overlooked man's spiritual qualities? Explain.

2. Do you agree with the author when he says, "There is only one reservation for Christians. Scientific knowledge must not contradict Scripture." Try to think of some ways in which science appears to disagree with Scripture.

3. Do you agree with the author's way of distinguishing between soul and spirit? Are these really different, or are soul and spirit the same?

4. How do you feel about Paul's statement in Romans 1:18–19 that man knows the truth

about God instinctively: How does this instinct manifest itself?

5. Scripture tells us that we are fulfilled through the Holy Spirit. Psychology says we are "self-actualized" by working our way through a series of steps that relate to our needs for survival, safety and security, belonging, and esteem. How do you feel about this? Can we be fulfilled without the Holy Spirit?

CHAPTER 11

Becoming a Christian

*You should not be surprised at my
saying, 'You must be born again.'*
JOHN 3:7

We are all born as children of God. We are created in His image. However, being God's child does not assure us that we will live in a close relationship with Him. In order for that to happen, we must be "born again." We must be transformed through acts of our own will and the power of the Holy Spirit.

On rare occasions such as the conversion of Saul, later known as Paul, God, Himself, initiates the change. The more typical experience involves going through a series of six steps in becoming a Christian, a process taking a few minutes or many years. These steps may occur in the order to be presented here, or we may go back and forth, repeating stages at several points in our journey. That's what happened to me. I kept repeating some of the steps time and time again. We know that God can deal with any of us in any manner He may wish; however, I believe that these stages are typical of what happens to most of us as we approach and go through Christian conversion.

1. Hearing the Word

2. Believing

3. Repentance

4. Commitment

5. Let Go and Let God

6. Rebirth

HEARING THE WORD

We cannot enter the Kingdom of Heaven if we have never heard of it or how to get there. Hearing the word is the first step toward salvation.

It is difficult to imagine that anyone growing up in the United States has not been exposed to the Gospel. Christianity has been a major part of our culture since the first settlers came to our shores early in the seventeenth century. They brought their religious beliefs with them and very early in our history these beliefs took shape in the development of churches, celebrations, and even in our schools. Our schools, at all levels from elementary through college, held religious teachings at the core of the curriculum. The earliest elementary schools were established for the primary purpose of teaching children to read the Bible and colleges were established to prepare young men for the ministry. Of course, these schools taught more than Bible reading and ministry preparation, but every person who attended school was exposed to these basics.

Even though our schools broadened the curriculum over the years, the Christian influence continued to be felt. I remember Bible reading, prayer, and the Pledge of Allegiance as a part of the daily routine in elementary school in the 1930s and the required Bible courses and chapel attendance in college. However, I didn't respond to those teachings, at least I didn't think I did. It was much later in life that I realized that seeds were planted during those years which finally took root and produced fruit.

The days are gone when we can depend on our public schools to provide an opportunity for our children to hear the Gospel message. That seems to be a sad and regrettable situation, and it is. But perhaps there is a blessing there also. If our children do not hear the Gospel message at school, we, the adults in the Christian community, must increase our efforts to teach them through our Sunday schools and church services, through exposure to Christian literature, television, and radio, and within our families.

We must also accept a greater responsibility for providing Christian witness not only to our children, but also throughout our community by the way we lead our daily lives. I can remember as a young adult wanting to talk to someone who was not a minister, but a lay person whose life reflected real Christian values. Those people were difficult to find. In fact, I cannot remember a single person whom I might characterize as my Christian mentor. That is a shame, and we should do everything in our power to keep that from happening to others. Don't be ashamed to let others know what you believe and what those beliefs have meant to you in your life.

The point is that we must witness in every way possible, and especially through the way we live our lives if others, including our children, are to hear and accept the Gospel. The seed must be sown before any fruit can be harvested.

BELIEVING

Hearing the Word is a necessary first step in becoming a Christian. However, hearing is not enough. In order to move on toward the goal of becoming a Christian, we must believe the Gospel message.

The accounts of the life of Jesus given in the four Gospels are not easy to believe. There is a great deal in those accounts that don't fit our usual way of experiencing the world. We are taught throughout our school years about the "natural" order of things. But we are not accustomed to virgin births, miraculous healings, walking on water, or returning from death. In order to believe these things, we must set aside much of what we have learned about nature and the natural way of things. We must accept the idea that God can, and does, intervene in nature at any time He may choose.

For me this was a tremendous hurdle to get over. I envied those who were able to just believe without having to analyze things according to the wisdom of the world. I wavered back and forth between believing and not believing.

I tried to explain things I did not believe by resorting to natural explanations. One convenient technique was to call the events I was having trouble with "parables." That way they didn't have to be literally true. In my mind, walking on water was like the parable of the Prodigal Son. I tried to explain events like raising people from the dead with the notion that they weren't really dead. It was convenient to deal with healings as merely relief from stress-induced symptoms. I tried to intellectualize the Gospels. That way I wouldn't have to throw them aside completely, but I could reshape them to conform to my way of thinking about the world. I even reached the point at one stage of my life that

I believed that we created God in our own image rather than the other way around.

Of course, these mind games that I was playing didn't really amount to believing. In fact, that way of dealing with the Bible put a barrier between me and the message God was attempting to convey. Belief involves accepting things as true, not twisting them to make them believable. But it must go beyond that. The kind of believing that leads us to becoming Christians goes beyond the mere acceptance of the Gospels as true. Believing must lead us to take action. It must be the kind of believing that makes a difference.

REPENTANCE

If we believe what we read in the four Gospels and the other New Testament writings, then we know that we are not perfect beings. In fact, we know we are sinful. We are aware that we fall short of being what God would want us to be. This first happened with Adam and Eve. God gave them a choice and they elected to disobey, to separate themselves from Him.

We see the same thing happening in the story of the Prodigal Son. The Son willingly separates himself from his father and in so doing begins to sink deeper and deeper into the worst conditions life has to offer. But this story goes beyond the story of Adam and Eve. We see in the account of the Prodigal Son that the father who allowed his son to go his own way continues to stand by, patiently awaiting his return. The son has only to recognize the error of his ways, turn around, and ask his father for forgiveness. Once the son has repented of his sins and returned home, he is fully accepted. No limitations are imposed, no accusations made. He is eagerly taken back into the household.

This is how it is for us. The nature of our relationship with God is repeated over and over again in Scripture. It applies to nations as well as to individuals. When the nation of Israel turned its back on God, He was always there to take them back when they wanted to return. When we turn from God, He continues to seek us out, not forcing us to return but always being there when we choose to come back. Once we recognize that we have separated ourselves from God, that we need Him, repent and ask for forgiveness, He takes us back. He always does that. That is a spiritual law.

From the Gospels we know that God's forgiveness is given to us [it is not earned] because Jesus bore the burden of our sins when He died on the cross. Without that act, there would be no forgiveness available to us. We certainly don't deserve it. And there are no other ways to accomplish this. In spite of the almost reverent attitude our society has for psychology, those who know the field well and are honest about what can and cannot be done through psychology will tell us that it cannot transform or take away our guilt. Only God can do that.

When we repent, we are transferring our burden of sin to Jesus who willingly takes it upon Himself, and in so doing frees us to return to the Father, along with Him.

It is only the act of repentance that really counts with God. He does not expect us to correct all of our mistakes and present ourselves perfect before Him. He knows we can't do that and He doesn't expect it. In fact, if you stop and think about it, if we could make ourselves perfect, I guess we wouldn't need Him. There would have been no need for Jesus' sacrifice, would there?

COMMITMENT

Repentance opens the door and God is waiting there to welcome us into His kingdom. But the journey has just begun. We are only inside the gate. We are also still in the real world, and we must cope with the pain and suffering to be found there. When God takes us in, He does not shelter us from the struggles we face in that world. We are not promised an easy life.

There is a marvelous parable found in three of the Gospels—Matthew, Mark, and Luke. It is usually referred to as the Parable of the Sower and it tells us what happens to seed when it is distributed over the ground by the sower. Some of the seed falls on harsh, unyielding, rocky soil and does not take root at all. We may be like that rocky soil when it comes to receiving the Word of God. We hear it, but reject it.

Then there is the seed that falls on poor, shallow soil. It takes root and grows, but soon withers and dies. We might be that way after hearing the Gospel message. There may be a burst of enthusiasm, but a just as rapid fading away. If the soil is not well prepared, is not rich and deep, this rapid withering can easily be the consequence. There is a lesson for us here regarding the early Christian education of our children.

Some of the seed takes root and grows well, but is eventually attacked and choked out by the weeds that may also grow in the same garden. Every Christian knows about this condition. There are forces all around us in the world working to choke us out. There are temptations of greed, vanity, and power which, if yielded to, will snuff out our faith. There are tragedies that cause us to question God's love and sometimes turn us away from Him.

Then, there is the seed that takes root and flourishes. Jesus tells us about that kind of seed:

"But the seed on good soil stands for those with a noble and good heart, who hear the word, retain it, and by persevering produce a crop." (Luke 8:15)

I added the underlining to emphasize that it is perseverance that allows this seed to fight off the forces of destruction and fulfill its potential. When we reject God or turn from Him we die. When we "hang in there" even when the going gets tough or we are faced with temptation, when we don't turn away from God, He stands with us through the battles and finally the victory is ours. This takes commitment, real commitment, and complete dedication. Without it we are like the seed that never blossoms or bears fruit. Without commitment, the Christian cannot survive.

LET GO AND LET GOD

Are you able to submit to the will of God, completely? Are you willing to give Him full control of all aspects of your life? This is, perhaps, the most difficult step of all in becoming a Christian. It is, however, clear that it is a step we must take. Jesus tells us over and over again that we must be able to do just that. We are not to worry about daily necessities (Matthew 6:25–33 and Luke 12:22–31), our family relationships (Matthew 10:37), or material things (Matthew 19:16–30, Mark 10:17–31, Luke 18:18–30).

Is Jesus saying we should just sit around doing nothing while God provides everything for us? Some of us seem to think so. When faced with a financial crisis, we expect God to arrange for us to win the lottery or get a large check from a long-lost uncle. Of course, such things do happen occasionally, but the Christian who has truly "Let go and let God" recognizes that he or she is an instrument of God's and may very well have to work very hard to overcome the obstacle that has presented itself. It has been my experience that God is much more likely to present me with opportunities to earn money than to give me a monetary gift. He is more likely to guide me in working through a personal relationship problem than to simply take care of things on His own.

Today we hear the phrase, "Go with the flow." The Christian goes with God's flow, which he knows from the study of Scripture, prayer, worship, and complete trust in the Lord. He knows that God is in control and will see him through. He may have to work hard, but he doesn't have to worry.

When we let God have control, we must be prepared to accept His way of handling things. Do we tend to ask God for a particular solution to a situation or do we ask God to provide His answer to the problem? Do I want God to heal me or to use me according to His will, even if it means I must continue to live with my infirmity or limitation? Should I ask God to see to it that this book is published or can I really turn this work over to Him to be used as He sees fit? If we are truly able to "Let go and let God," we will be confident and trusting in His handling of such matters.

We have had an experience that may help illustrate this. My wife, Nancy, was working in a job which she liked very much and which was important to her. She had gone into the position under difficult circumstances and, according to all of the feedback she received, she was doing quite well. The entire situation made her feel valued and appreciated. In addition, she became friends with a

Christian lady who she was able to help on two very important personal matters. This friend often said that she knew God sent Nancy to her. Everything seemed to be going well. Then some changes were made on the job that changed things drastically. Instead of feeling valued and appreciated, she began to feel the sting of frequent criticism. The reasons for the criticisms were unclear. Nancy prayed that these on-the-job problems would be resolved. But matters got progressively worse until there was no choice but to leave. At first it felt like a crushing defeat, being pushed out of a job that had meant so much to her.

But then a strange thing happened. She began to see how leaving the job and going into retirement made more time available to the two of us. We began to do things together that we had not been able to do before. She had more time for our son who was going through a difficult situation in his life. Finally, it became clear that maybe her friend was right. She had not been in that job for herself at all, but because God had needed her there to help her friend through the crisis in her life.

When all of this happened it seemed, at first, that perhaps God didn't care. He wasn't working things out in a way that would keep her in her job. Was He letting her be hurt for some reason we couldn't understand? Or was He working things out according to His own plan?

Sometimes the pain we feel may come when we

are trying to control a situation in a manner that is not God's way. We may be determined to have things work out the way *we* want them to work out. Then God comes up with a solution that is far better than ours and totally different from anything we had thought of. This sort of thing happens to Christians all the time. When we can come to realize that if we relinquish control to God, He will see us safely through, then we can give up the pain and worry. As Christians, we must truly "Let go and let God." Never forget:

"For we know that in all things God works for the good of those who love him, who have been called according to his purpose." (Romans 8:28)

REBIRTH

If you and I can honestly and sincerely go through these steps toward becoming a Christian, the final stage will happen automatically. If, after hearing the Word, we believe, repent, make a commitment, and then completely place our trust in the Lord, we will experience a rebirth. The Holy Spirit will come to us and a transformation will begin to take place.

Once you have been reborn in the Spirit, once the Holy Spirit has taken control of your life, things begin to change for you. For some, the changes occur rapidly. For others, the rebirth is the beginning of a transformation that will take place over time, perhaps even a lifetime. Even Paul struggled for years:

"I do not understand what I do. For what I want to do I do not do, but what I hate I do. And if I do what I do not want to do, I agree that the law is good. As it is, it is no longer I myself who do it, but it is sin living in me. I know that nothing good lives in me, that is, in my sinful nature. For I have the desire to do what is good, but I cannot carry it out. For what I do is not the good I want to do; no, the evil I do not want to do - this I keep on doing .Now if I do what I do not want to do, it is no longer I who do it, but it is sin living in me that does it. So I find this law at work: When I want to do good, evil is right there with me. For in my inner being I delight in God's law; but I see another law at work in the members of my body, waging war against the law of my mind and making me a prisoner of the law of sin at work within my members. What a wretched man I am! Who will rescue me from this body of death? Thanks be to God—through Jesus Christ our Lord!"

ROMANS 7:15–25

Most of us are probably like Paul. We know we are on the right path but it seems that the struggle will never end. Much like Jacob, we are wrestling with an angel (Genesis 32:24–26) in a battle we actually want to lose.

This happens because we are human and because it is difficult for us to completely surrender our lives to God, even when we want to. We struggle back and forth. Even Jesus had His moment of resistance in the Garden of Gesthemane. Though He knew what He had to do, even He asked if He could be relieved of the burden. As in Jesus' situation, God's will is always going to prevail and by losing control, we win.

You can tell if you are a Christian by observing how you are handling conflict between the old and the new natures. The Christian may have moments when it would be easiest to exercise that awesome power of choice that God gave us and just walk away, give in to the pressure, follow the crowd. But he cannot do that. As soon as he turns his back on God, he feels pulled to return to the battle. He can't give up. But God will continue to stand by. He is there for everyone. God will still be there and, in the long run, win the battle. The Holy Spirit will take control of you and you will win by losing.

A Test

We are now ready to return to the question: "Am I a Christian?" Here's a little test for you:

- Do you believe that Jesus is the Son of God, your Savior?

- Do you need salvation and have you trusted in God's grace to provide this?

- Do you recognize and acknowledge your sinfulness and truly repent of your sins?

- Is God the central and controlling force in your life?

- Do you trust God in all things?

- Have you experienced the transforming power of the Holy Spirit?

- Are you, with the Holy Spirit, fighting and winning the battle against your old sinful nature?

Only you can answer these questions truthfully and you and God know if you are really a Christian. I sincerely hope that you are. And if you are, you know that there are many difficult issues that you must deal with every day of your life. In his great Christian classic, *The Pilgrim's Progress*, John Bunyan makes this abundantly clear. In the book Christian enters the gate and is relieved of his burden within the first few pages. But his walk has just begun. He faces obstacles and questions at every turn. We are the same. As Christians, we are concerned about our

Bible study, worship, and stewardship, along with many other questions about this world we live in, our relationship to God, and the way Satan tries to work his wiles on us. I invite you to join me in examining these and others issues of concern in the chapters ahead.

SOME QUESTIONS FOR THOUGHT AND DISCUSSION

1. How do the stages in becoming a Christian presented here fit with your own experience?

2. Are some of the steps harder to work through than others? If you believe this is the case, which steps are the easiest, which the most difficult? Why?

3. At which point in the process of becoming a Christian do you feel the person is "saved?"

4. Does the Parable of the Sower teach us that we can be saved and then lose our salvation because of the "weeds and thorns" we encounter in real life?

5. After studying and discussing this chapter, do you feel that most of us who claim to be Christians are entitled to that name or are there actually only a few real Christians?

CHAPTER III

A New Person

*"A good tree cannot bear bad fruit, and a bad tree
cannot bear good fruit. Every tree that does not
bear good fruit is cut down and thrown into the
fire. Thus, by their fruit you will recognize them."*
MATTHEW 7:18–20

What is the Holy Spirit? I wrestled with that question for many years before learning the answer through personal experience. I could never figure it out intellectually. When I tried to do that, I consistently ran into a brick wall. The whole idea of a Holy Spirit seemed so vague and abstract that I just couldn't come to grips with it. But then, perhaps that is the secret. We cannot know the Holy Spirit until we let Him in and once we do that, the answer becomes obvious.

The Holy Spirit provides a connection that brings together spirit, soul, and body to create a whole and complete person. This step releases the power of that spirit of God that is already in us. Instead of being a quiet and subdued sense of God's presence, this spirit becomes a dynamic force affecting every aspect of our lives. The closest I can come to a "natural" event that is somewhat similar is the action of adrenaline in our bodies. Most of the time, the adrenaline is just stored in our adrenal glands. When something happens that causes us to become emotionally aroused the adrenaline is released, empowering us to react more quickly and with greater strength than we normally have. The adrenaline has been there all along but it takes a special event to release that power so we can use it to deal with the situation with which we are confronted. Similarly, allowing the Holy Spirit into your soul empowers the spirit to affect the way you act and think in a very real and forceful way. The difference is that the adrenaline effect will harm you if it is allowed to persist for too long a time. The spiritual power released by the Holy Spirit will never harm you. Instead, it will change you in marvelous ways that will remain with you forever, if you will allow it. Also, adrenaline serves an immediate and limited purpose. Spiritual power affects everything you do and think. All of your priorities are shifted away from being world centered to being God centered. You truly, "Let Go and Let God." You are now in the world but not of the world.

It is only through the power of the Holy Spirit that this change can happen. You cannot do it by yourself. Furthermore, you have Satan on your back resisting any attempt you might make on your own using the natural part of your soul. It is only through the power of the Holy Spirit that you can connect spirit, soul, and body and become whole. When the Holy Spirit does take control of your life, some very special things will begin to happen to you.

Once the Holy Spirit became a part of my life, the Bible, inspirational books, films, and media programming took on a whole new meaning. A thirst for the Word emerged in a way that was totally different from anything I had experienced in the past. The Bible had been something I knew I should read and study, but reading it didn't really have any meaningful impact on my life. I usually ended up just being bored or questioning the truthfulness of much of what I read. I tried to make the Bible fit into the "natural" way of looking at life that had been so deeply ingrained in me from early childhood. I wondered how such a book could have survived and been at the top of the best seller list for many centuries. It lay around the house, but was read only on those rare occasions when my curiosity was aroused or when I felt guilty about not reading it.

I remember so clearly my amazement at the change that came over a friend some years ago when he invited the Holy Spirit into his life. As a history teacher, he had gone out of his way to criticize the authenticity of much of the content of the Bible. He openly criticized students who believed in the truth of the Scriptures. In his own way, he persecuted believers. Then, virtually overnight, he changed. He would come into the office bursting to talk about some passage of Scripture he had been reading. In every spare moment, I would find him studying, relating what he had read to some issue in his life. And within a few months he decided to give up his teaching career and enter a seminary to prepare for the ministry. I often think of him in relation to Paul. The transformation from persecutor to disciple was so dramatic, so total, that it seemed unbelievable. But there it was, happening before my eyes. I recall asking him one day if the Bible was a miraculous book, and, of course, he said that it was. I wondered why it didn't seem so to me.

I now know why. It was the Holy Spirit that made all of the difference. He is the key. Things I read, films I watched, and music I listened to took on new meaning. The Bible began to speak personally and vividly. It was no longer hard to believe. The truths it reveals became clear and profound in their influence on my life. It guided and it comforted. Sometimes it shook me up by obliging me to rethink some of my attitudes and actions. It is truly a miraculous book.

PRAYER

For many years my prayers consisted mainly of asking God for help, ritual repetitions in church services, and grace at meals sometimes, but never in public. Can you imagine why I might have been skeptical about people who claimed their prayers were answered? Mine hardly ever seemed to be.

The Holy Spirit changed all of that. The first thing I noticed was that I would be chatting with Jesus in prayer. It was much like having a talk with a friend. There were no fancy phrases, just talking and then listening for His reply. Can you imagine what many of my psychology colleagues think of that? "Sure, you talk to Jesus." That's what I would have said a few years ago to anyone making the claim I'm making to you now. Until it happens to you, you just can't believe it. It's not natural.

The second thing I noticed was that prayers were being answered. We, along with several members of our church, had a prayer group that met in our home. We kept a weekly record of our prayer requests. It seemed to make our prayers more specific and powerful when we put our concerns in writing. Then, each week we talked about the situations that we had been praying about. The things that happened just boggle the mind. There have been physical healings and restored relationships. God has responded to financial needs and to situations in our church. This has all happened within a few months. No telling what long-range answers He has in store for us.

The phrase, "praying in the Spirit" is often understood to mean the same thing as "speaking in tongues." This, however, is a misunderstanding.

Speaking in tongues occurs during public worship and is closely associated with prophecy.

When we pray in the Spirit, our prayers should be private and are mainly prayers of praise and thanksgiving. There is a definite shift from praying "for this" and "for that" to prayers that praise God not only for the blessings we have received, but also for the mountains we have to climb. It is easy to be thankful for healings, the receipt of unexpected money, or the birth of a healthy child. It is not so easy to give thanks and praise for a child who is severely handicapped. Yet that is just what happens. All things are seen as being under God's control and part of His plan. Paul talks about praying in the Spirit in the eighth chapter of Romans:

> In the same way, the Spirit helps us in our weakness. We do not know what we ought to pray for, but the Spirit himself intercedes for us with groans that words cannot express. And he who searches our hearts knows the mind of the Spirit, because the Spirit intercedes for the saints in accordance with God's will.
>
> ROMANS 8:26–27

The Spirit takes nothing away from my prayer life, but adds so much.

THE PEACE THAT PASSES
ALL UNDERSTANDING

The Holy Spirit came into my life in the summer of 1991. He entered my soul during a time of great financial stress. My income for the summer had just been cut drastically compared to previous summers, an engine blew up in our car, we had just experienced losses of thousands of dollars in real estate investments, and in a few weeks I was going to lose even more income. And Nancy would, too, as a result of her illness. We were worried and upset. It was just about then that the Holy Spirit took over. We decided it was time to take God's promises seriously and we knew the only way to do that was with the help of the Holy Spirit. We read in the book of James:

"In the same way, faith by itself, if it is not accompanied by action, is dead." (James 2:17)

And it took the Holy Spirit to push us into action, to turn faith into works. What happened was that in the midst of financial disaster, we began to tithe. Now, I'm not going to tell you that an unknown rich uncle died and left us a fortune or that Ed McMahon showed up with a check for a million dollars. In fact, stories that tell of people beginning to tithe and then receiving large sums of money from unexpected sources trouble me somewhat.

Stories of that sort tend to suggest that the reason for tithing is to make money. They may lead us to believe that our gifts to God will always be repaid many times over with money. Actually, the promises of abundance given to us by God do not necessarily refer to financial abundance. God's gifts may touch us in so many other areas of life.

What did happen was that we stopped *worrying* about finances. Things were still not easy. For most folks problems never completely go away in this hectic, complex and greed driven world in which we live. But the promise is not freedom from the world's tribulations. It is freedom from worry. That's the peace that Jesus promised. And we stand on that promise:

"And we know that in all things God works for the good of those who love him, who have been called according to his purpose." (Romans 8:28)

We know that things will be taken care of according to God's plan so long as we love Him and give Him control of our lives.

But this does not mean that we are to sit back and do nothing. God has given each of us talents and abilities and He expects us to use them to the very best of our ability. That is one of the ways we glorify Him. This is made very clear in the following passage from Colossians:

"Whatever you do, work at it with all your heart, as working for the Lord, not for men ... " (Colossians 3:23)

For more evidence that God expects us to help ourselves we look to the book of James:

"Do not merely listen to the word, and so deceive yourselves. Do what it says." (James 1:22)

What this all means is that so long as we love God and are His children, and we use the talents He has given us in ways that glorify Him, we don't have to worry about our needs being met. He will direct us. He will set us straight if we head down the wrong path. But we must be prepared to do things God's way. Sometimes He leads us in ways we would never go on our own. We must trust and we must believe. And if we do, we can go ahead with the assurance that all things will be done according to His will and plan.

God's Secret Wisdom

Has the Holy Spirit become a part of you? Have you invited the Holy Spirit to take control of your soul, your spirit, and your body? Give yourself a little test. Read the second chapter of I Corinthians. Pay special attention to verses six through ten. Here is what it says:

> We do, however, speak a message of wisdom among the mature, but not the wisdom of this age or of the rulers of this age, who are coming to nothing. No, we speak of God's secret wisdom, a wisdom that has been hidden and that God destined for our glory before time began. None of the rulers of this age understood it, for if they had, they

would not have crucified the Lord of glory.
However, as it is written "No eye has seen, no
ear has heard, no mind has conceived what
God has prepared for those who love him"
but God has revealed it to us by his Spirit.

1 CORINTHIANS 2:6–10

Do you know "God's Secret Wisdom?" What is
Paul talking about here? You can know this wisdom
only if the Holy Spirit is part of you. Verse ten tells us
that. If the story of Jesus' life, crucifixion, and resurrection seem like foolishness to you, if you cannot understand the power of greatness of the gospel story, then
perhaps you have not really let the Holy Spirit take
control. Because, you see, the story of Jesus is foolishness if you are only able to see it through worldly eyes.
It is only with the power of the Holy Spirit that we
can see beyond the world's limited view and into the
heart and mind of God. This ability to discern is one
of the characteristics of those who have the fruit of the
Spirit, ours for the asking.

LOVE

The fruit of the Spirit takes many forms. But we cannot leave this subject without discussing the greatest
of the fruits, love. The beautiful thirteenth chapter
of I Corinthians makes this very clear. This is a text
we should all read regularly.

When we read in the Gospels that Jesus taught
that we should love everyone, even our enemies,

we see that this is an extremely hard lesson. It is a wonderful sentiment, a beautiful thought, but can it really be done? Is it possible to love someone who is trying to hurt you or your loved ones? Can you truly love someone who steals from you? Can you separate the acts that people sometimes carry out, acts that you despise, from the persons themselves? Can we see every human being as a potential prodigal son? Regardless of how far that person may have strayed can we welcome him or her home, leaving all judgment to God.

That is what God wants of us. In the thirteenth chapter of I Corinthians we read:

> Love is patient, love is kind. It does not envy,
> it does not boast, it is not proud. It is not rude,
> it is not self-seeking, it is not easily angered,
> it keeps no record of wrongs. Love does not
> delight in evil but rejoices with the truth. It
> always protects, always trusts, always hopes,
> always perseveres. Love never fails.
>
> I CORINTHIANS 13:4–8

Apply that standard of love to the most unlovable person you can think of. Can you imagine loving that person in God's way just on your own? Won't it take the Holy Spirit to make that kind of loving possible? The exciting thing is that the Holy Spirit can, indeed, allow you to love in that way that is impossible if we rely only on our natural abilities. He will give us the means to do it.

God the Father, God the Son, God the Holy Spirit; God in all of His manifestations, has touched my life in so many ways. Just exactly how He will touch you depends on your needs and God's plan for your life. We can't know the specific blessings or the trials God might have in store for us. What we can be sure of, however, is that things will start happening once we let the Holy Spirit in. We have looked at some of these, but now let's look at one more—the transformation of our lives. When the Holy Spirit takes over your life, you will change. You will start becoming a new kind of person. In an earlier chapter we examined the characteristics of "natural man" described by Paul in Galatians. Let's look at those verses again:

> The acts of the sinful nature are obvious: sexual immorality, impurity and debauchery; idolatry and witchcraft; hatred, discord, jealousy, fits of rage, selfish ambition, dissensions, factions and envy; drunkenness, orgies, and the like.
>
> GALATIANS 5:19–21

It is not only the Bible that tells us that we are afflicted with traits such as these. The unhappy outcome of many studies in psychology has been to document the picture Paul has painted for us here. Psychology tells us that when we remove the restraints placed on us by society, many of us become very much like the person Paul describes. When away from home at a vacation spot, a place where we are not known, do we sometimes behave in ways we would never act if we thought we might be recognized? Do we conform to social pressure, the ways of the world, even when doing so might go against our sense of right and wrong? Might we do things when we believe we are hidden in a crowd that we would not do if we were alone and clearly recognizable? Psychology tells us that many of us would have to answer, yes, to questions like these.

This idea that we are badly flawed is very prevalent in our society. There is a widespread notion that we all need help. We need help inside; help that will change this "nature" into something more positive. And we need help outside; help in coping with what seems to be an increasingly complex and stressful world.

When science and Scripture agree so clearly on an issue as they do on this question of the nature of natural man, we can be certain we are onto something solid. And in this case, the conclusion from both psychology and the Bible is that in our natural condition, we are not very nice. We are not at all what we think we would like to be.

While psychology can demonstrate the presence of these unfavorable characteristics, it can offer little in the way of help in bringing about change. Psychology falls far short of fulfilling the claims made on its behalf. But don't take my word for it.

Read *The Shrinking of America*, by Bernie Zilbergeld. You will soon learn that many of the claims made on behalf of psychology as a transforming agent cannot be substantiated.

In spite of this evidence, psychology, the American public, and Scripture express a belief in the possibility of change. When I asked my students if they had ever experienced a spontaneously occurring, deep-seated change in some aspect of their personalities, or if they know anyone to whom this has happened, an overwhelming majority answer, yes.

But how does this happen? Psychology doesn't have a good answer. Can we get any help from the Bible?

Paul tells us very directly and specifically how to bring about this transformation:

> But the fruit of the Spirit is love, joy, peace, patience, kindness, goodness, faithfulness, gentleness and self-control. Against such things there is no law. Those who belong to Christ Jesus have crucified the sinful nature with its passions and desires. Since we live by the Spirit, let us keep in step with the Spirit.
>
> GALATIANS 5:22–25

These qualities that are quite different from those possessed by the natural man are the fruit of the Spirit, the Holy Spirit. The Spirit is the power that transforms the sinful nature into the person described above. Psychology cannot recognize this power because the Holy Spirit operates beyond the reach of science. Psychology, as a science, is limited to studying natural laws. But because psychology cannot "see" the spiritual world does not mean it does not exist. Our eyes cannot see certain light rays, but they are there. Our ears cannot hear certain sound ranges, but they are there. The fact that science cannot see things is not proof that those things don't exist. But you already knew that, didn't you?

I'm going to raise a question here that may have already occurred to you. Are you thinking that you know people who seem to be patient, good, kind, loving and all of those other things Paul described as fruit of the Spirit who are not Christians? How could they be that sort of person?

We are all born with the sinful nature described by Paul. From the moment we are created, these forces become a part of the kind of person we are. As a result of the kind of teaching we receive from birth onward, we may learn that to act out these basic urges can be harmful to ourselves and to others. We are taught that these behaviors are bad. We need to curb our tendency to act in ways that are not in accord with the values and standards of our culture. If our urge is to engage in sexual behavior that is considered immoral, we can resist the temptation to carry out that urge. If expressing our anger would lead to behavior that is against the law, we may very well restrain ourselves. If being impatient or unkind might result in feelings of guilt or shame, we might learn patience and kindness. Our conscience, in other words, becomes a force that inhibits the carrying out of our natural tendencies. Those undesirable qualities are still there, we just learn not to act on them, especially when doing so might result in some harm to ourselves. We can learn to be self-disciplined.

Some who call themselves Christians are "being good" because they believe that God is watching them and grading their behavior. These folks are behaving themselves because they are concerned with being caught, not because their nature has changed.

The difference for the spirit-filled Christian is two-fold. Once the Holy Spirit takes control of our soul, we keep whatever learned controls on our behavior we may have acquired. But we also experience a change in our nature and a power that directs us and touches every part of our being.

In writing to the Christians in Rome about the changes that take place when one becomes a follower of Christ, Paul said this:

> But thanks be to God that, though you used to be slaves to sin, you wholeheartedly obeyed the form of teaching to which you were entrusted. You have been set free from sin and have become slaves to righteousness.
>
> ROMANS 6:17–18

To the person who has not let go and let God, the sinful nature is still the controlling force. Even when that person is being good or calling him or herself a Christian, there is always that tendency to drift back to the old nature. On the other hand, Spirit-filled Christians are slaves to righteousness, which has become the controlling force in our lives. When the Christian drifts away, or backslides, the Holy Spirit immediately lets him know of the transgression and turns him back to righteousness.

In summary, we can say that the fruit of the Spirit that comes to all believers who invite the Holy Spirit into their lives include:

1. A thirst for knowing God and a new ability to discern God's message for us.

2. An enriched and more powerful prayer experience.

3. The peace that passeth all understanding.

4. Knowledge of God's secret wisdom.

5. A greater capacity for love.

6. A transformation of one's personality.

There is all of this and so much more.

SOME QUESTIONS FOR THOUGHT AND DISCUSSION

1. How do you feel about the author's statement that one cannot understand the Holy Spirit intellectually, that we can know the Spirit only through experiencing Him?

2. How does your experience compare to the author's regarding the impact of the Holy Spirit on your Bible study and prayer life?

3. Do you believe that the Holy Spirit empowers you to deal with the problems of life with assurance and confidence or do you expect the Holy Spirit to take care of problems for you?

4. Why would the author say that the Gospel story is foolishness when seen through the eyes of the world?

5. Do you feel that the transformation in our nature that is brought on by the Holy Spirit happens instantaneously or is it something that goes on through our lifetime?

CHAPTER IV

Gifts of the Spirit

To one there is given through the Spirit the message of wisdom, to another the message of knowledge by means of the same Spirit, to another faith by the same Spirit, to another gifts of healing by that one Spirit, to another miraculous powers, to another prophecy, to another distinguishing between spirits, to another speaking in different kinds of tongues, and to still another the interpretation of tongues. All these are the work of one and the same Spirit and he gives them to each one, just as he determines.

1 CORINTHIANS 12:8–11

We know that the fruit of the Spirit comes to every believer in Jesus Christ through the Holy Spirit. But the Holy Spirit brings more. Paul tells us that in addition to the fruit, we receive what are called the gifts of the Spirit. We may be blessed with:

- The Message of Wisdom
- The Message of Knowledge
- Faith
- Gift of Healing
- Miraculous Powers
- Prophecy
- Distinguishing Between Spirits
- Speaking in Different Kinds of Tongues
- Interpretation of Tongues

Let's examine each of theses gifts, and then consider who may receive them and how they are to be used.

The Message of Wisdom

The American Heritage Dictionary tells us that wisdom is "understanding of what is true, right, or lasting."

In the life of the Christian, there are numerous

occasions when "understanding what is true, right, or lasting" is vitally important. These occasions may involve making decisions regarding the business and activities of the church, or they may relate to some more personal issues. As we think about those times when we have been faced with making particularly difficult choices, we may recall how often someone was there who seemed to sense the essence of the problem and just how to proceed. More than that, we know that if we followed that advice, things usually turned out well.

We can find no better model to illustrate the gifts of the Spirit than Jesus Himself. Time and again, when He was challenged by the religious leaders of His day, He was able to see beyond the superficiality of their questions and focus on the spiritual truth in the issues they raised with Him.

> But the Pharisees and the teachers of the law who belonged to their sect complained to his disciples, "Why do you eat and drink with tax collectors and sinners?" Jesus answered them, "It is not the healthy who need a doctor, but the sick. I have not come to call the righteous, but sinners to repentance."
>
> LUKE 5:30–31

We will not find anyone among our acquaintances with the wisdom of Jesus, but we do find those who seem to be more gifted than most in this regard. Their kind of wisdom comes from the Holy Spirit.

THE MESSAGE OF KNOWLEDGE

Are you amazed at how much some people seem to know about the Bible? You may have been a dutiful student of Scripture for years, a Sunday school regular, yet you cannot hold a candle to these folks when it comes to questions of what is in the Bible and where it is located. And the gift referred to as the message of knowledge does not just apply to knowledge of the Bible. It could cover any kind of knowledge that might be used to glorify God such as knowledge of the workings of the church, or the history of some group of people. One might be gifted with vast knowledge of the universe, of atoms and electrons, or of the creatures that make up God's creation.

Jesus possessed this gift and demonstrated it most often through His knowledge of Scripture, and He chided the Sadducees when they asked Him about the responsibility of brothers regarding the widow of one of the brothers.

"Jesus replied, 'You are in error because you do not know the Scriptures or the power of God.'" (Matthew 22:29)

The gifts of knowledge and wisdom are closely related, but are not the same thing. One may have great knowledge, but have difficulty applying it wisely. Or one might be infinitely wise, but have only a small reservoir of knowledge. In the best of all worlds, those who possess the gifts of the Spirit work together in harmony, each sharing what he does best.

FAITH

All of us who are Christians have faith. Without it we could not believe in a God we cannot know by using our five senses. Faith, according to the writer of the book of Hebrews :"... *is being sure of what we hope for and certain of what we do not see.* "(Hebrews 11:1) Most certainly the hopes of Christians for now and for eternity are closely tied to our God whom we cannot see, feel, smell, taste or hear in a direct and sure way. By this I do not mean that we aren't aware of God's presence at times. We even hear Him speak to us but these are not experiences that prove conclusively that God is there. We can't prove the existence of God scientifically but we don't have to. We believe in Him by faith. More than that; we know He is with us. That's all we need to know. We don't need any proof beyond that. That's faith.

Faith is more than that. The fruit of the Spirit includes faithfulness. Once the Holy Spirit has become a part of us, we are committed to God and with the help of the Holy Spirit we remain committed to Him. Thus, we have the faith to believe and the faithfulness to remain loyal and true through all of life's ups and downs.

What then, is the gift of faith given by the Holy Spirit? If we are all faithful by virtue of being saved, don't we all have the gift? And the answer to that question is no. If we are saved we are faithful, but we are also human and subject to the weaknesses that go with being human. Let's remember Peter. In spite of the close bond he had with Jesus he gave in to pressure and denied Him. At that point in his life he was like most of us. He had faith and he had devoted his life to following Jesus, but even he had a breaking point. His faith was a somewhat fragile thing. Remember when Peter stepped out of the boat and took a few steps on the water? But his faith faded and he began to sink. Peter had faith but not the gift of faith at that time.

Those with the gift of faith have a faith that is unshakeable. No circumstances can break the tie they have with God, even for a moment. We believe that eventually Peter received the gift and remained true through the most trying times. From the Old Testament we know of Abraham, Noah, Job, Daniel and his three companions who were tortured in Nebuchadnezzar's court. We know the story of Joseph in Egypt. These were all giants of faith. In our modern age the name of Billy Graham stands out as one who has remained fully committed and faithful throughout his life. No doubt there are many others whose faith far exceeds that of most of us. And as it is with all of the gifts of the Spirit, those who are so blessed have a duty to use that gift to glorify God in some special way.

GIFT OF HEALING

The granting of the gift of healing is a very special event. Jesus demonstrated this gift often in His ministry and any of us who are alert to watch for such things will see that miraculous healings continue to happen around us today. People's bodies are healed when medical science says they cannot be healed. People's lives are transformed when psychology says that transformation is not possible. At times, Mother Nature acts in ways that are contrary to the natural laws which govern her usual behavior.

We are sometimes inclined to believe that all of our doctors have the gift of healing. That's not so. Some do, but certainly not all. Doctors are trained in the science of medicine and in many cases people are cured through the use of scientific techniques. However, there are some physicians who go beyond relying solely on science and we can recognize them. First of all, they love the Lord. They are believers. This means that in their practice they manifest the qualities of discipleship. They love God and they love their patients, who are their neighbors. They pray for and with their patients. Of course, all of their patients are not miraculously healed. But when that does happen they are not surprised and they do not reach for some far-fetched explanation for the miracle. They rejoice with the one who is healed. We are blessed to have three such doctors in our lives: Alessio Salsano, our internist; Wilkins Hubbard, our surgeon; and John DiAmelio, our podiatrist. These truly gifted physicians will be the first to remind the healed patient of the source of the healing and the responsibility the patient has to determine for what purpose God has made him whole.

MIRACULOUS POWERS

The granting of the gift of miraculous powers is a rare and very special event. Jesus demonstrated this gift often in His ministry and if we keep our eyes open to such things we will see that miracles continue to happen. Sometimes there is an individual at the center of things who has caused the event to occur. When the Israelites left Egypt headed for the land of the Canaanites they took the way that led them to the edge of the Red Sea. The Egyptians, who were determined to capture them and return them to Egypt, followed closely. Finally, with the Red Sea ahead of them and the army of Pharoah behind them:

> Then Moses stretched out his hand over the sea, and all that night the Lord drove the sea back with a strong east wind and turned it into dry land. The waters were divided, and the Israelites went through the sea on dry ground, with a wall of water on their right and on their left.
>
> EXODUS 14:21–22

Moses was God's agent in this miracle which resulted in freeing the Israelites from bondage in Egypt.

Miraculous events happened often in Moses' life. Usually, however, this particular gift seems to be not for a lifetime, but in connection with a special event . It may be a moment of insight, quickness, or strength which results in a miraculous outcome, never to be repeated. Miracles are not everyday events. We should not expect them to be and we should not expect an individual who is an instrument of God in the performance of one miracle to repeat the performance on a regular basis. I would beware of anyone claiming to be a miracle worker unless I could see the hand of God at work in his life.

PROPHECY

We usually think of the word prophesy in reference to seeing into the future. The Bible is filled with accounts of just such prophesies. But the word prophecy also has other meanings, very complex meanings, which make this one of the most difficult of all of the gifts of the Holy Spirit to understand.

The Bible teaches us that prophesy may take several forms;—interpretation of present events, prediction of events yet to occur, and communication of God's messages to His people. A prophet may carry out any of these roles, but those who are truly gifted by the Holy Spirit are most likely to combine all three of these functions in their work.

Regardless of the prophets' messages or styles, those who are God's true prophets share some things in common. First, they have all had a direct and personal contact with God who endowed the gift and the responsibilities that go with the gift. The prototype prophet, Moses, received his charge from God when he encountered God through the burning bush. Isaiah's lips were touched in his dramatic confrontation with God. Everyone who is truly a prophet has met God face-to-face.

God's prophets don't just foretell future events. Through the power of the Holy Spirit, the true prophet sees through time barriers and unites the past, present, and future by sensing how God has bound time together. That which is past, that which is now, and that which is to come are all part of one plan and the true prophet has a sense of the unity of that plan.

Thus, the prophet is more a revealer of God than a predictor of the future. He is God's messenger to His people. Others may make accurate predictions, but simply anticipating future events alone does not authenticate a prophet. Only when the prophet's message is a revelation of God Himself can we accept it as true.

The gift of prophecy includes a special form of communication between God and His prophets. This ability is often confused with "speaking in tongues."

Read the fourteenth chapter of I Corinthians very carefully and prayerfully. You will see that though prophecy and speaking in tongues are closely related, they are not the same thing. The prophet speaks in a special way with God, but that is not the language to be used in conveying God's message to His people. The special language is private and must be interpreted in order to be understood by the public.

We must beware those who claim this gift but are, in fact, false prophets. They are inclined to dramatic pronouncements regarding such matters as Christ's return and the end of the world. Scripture is quite explicit here, telling us that no man knows when events of this kind will take place. After speaking at some length about the final days and the signs of the end of the age, Christ says,

"No one knows about that day or hour, not even the angels in heaven, nor the Son, but only the Father." *(Matthew 24:36)*

Nevertheless, we are constantly bombarded by predictions. These pronouncements are made over and over, particularly when a new century approaches, but they are always wrong. These events will take place when God determines to do it, and He is not going to tell us ahead of time. You and I simply need to always be prepared.

DISTINGUISHING BETWEEN SPIRITS

Can you always distinguish between good and evil? The ability to recognize whether the source of prophecy or pronouncement is truly God or an evil spirit is a special gift of the Holy Spirit. Most of us probably feel that we possess this gift. We believe we can recognize good and bad, right and wrong, truth and falsehood. But history would prove us wrong. Time and again large groups of caring, committed Christians are led astray by false teachers. Cultists such as Jim Jones and David Koresh have developed large followings. But it isn't just those in cults who are led astray. At one time or another, most of us have found ourselves headed in some misguided direction after taking the advice of someone we trusted and believed to be a messenger of truth. The pattern was repeated over and over again in the Old Testament accounts of how God's people drifted away again. The New Testament warns of the influence of false teachers. Even though it is easy for us to believe we will not be fooled, the chances are we could be.

It is when we are hurting the most, in our time of greatest need, that we are most vulnerable to those who might misguide or take advantage of us. We do not always see clearly during times of stress. In fact, only a few of us are truly gifted with the ability to distinguish between God and the spirits of evil. We need to learn to recognize those special, gifted individuals and listen to the messages they bring to us.

SPEAKING IN DIFFERENT KINDS OF TONGUES

This gift is an absolute necessity for those who would minister to people of cultures and languages other than their own. I cannot imagine a foreign missionary being successful without this gift. It was first manifest on the day of Pentecost when the apostles were able to communicate with people from various lands and languages and still have their message understood. This ability, the ability to cut through barriers of language and still communicate effectively, is what speaking in different kinds of tongues refers to.

There appears to be some confusion among Christians regarding this gift. Some use the phrase "speaking in tongues" to mean the manifestation of a form of utterances believed to be a heavenly or angelic kind of communication, sometimes associated with the gift of prophecy. There are others who believe that the sounds made are, in fact, some ancient, dead language. A friend who had the experience was told he was speaking in an old, forgotten Egyptian dialect. (It was not clear how the listener was able to recognize the utterances as coming from a forgotten language.) These rather esoteric interpretations of "tongues" have been the basis of division and strife in the church from the earliest days. In the fourteenth chapter of I Corinthians Paul chastises the church members of his day regarding the misuse and misunderstanding of this phenomenon. Today churches are being divided by those Christians who see this ability as a sign of special favor from the Holy Spirit, or the absence of "tongues" as a sign that those who do not have the gift are lesser Christians.

Actually Scripture seems to suggest that it is those with the gift of prophecy who are most likely to experience this unusual phenomenon of language. It is the medium through which they communicate privately with God. It is not a language to be used in public display. Look again at the fourteenth chapter of I Corinthians, especially verses 18 through 25. It seems clear that when Paul refers to the gift of speaking in different kinds of tongues, he is referring to the ability to communicate the gospel across language barriers. Speaking in heavenly tongues is related to the gift of prophecy and is to be used only in one's private conversations with God, not in public display.

INTERPRETATION OF TONGUES

The gift of interpretation of tongues is the other end of the communication of one speaking in tongues. There must be a speaker and a hearer for any communication to be effective. I could write the second best book ever written, but if no one reads it, there is no communication. So it is with speaking in tongues. If no one understands what is said, no message is conveyed.

Paul said that speaking in tongues is a gift to be used publicly in trying to reach unbelievers, which might include unbelievers with various language backgrounds. There must be someone among them who can understand and interpret. (Take note that this interpreter may be an unbeliever who is being used by the Holy Spirit at that moment to do God's work.) The interpreter understands the message of the speaker and translates into familiar language forms.

It must be emphasized that the gifts of the Spirit, unlike the fruit of the Spirit, are not all given to every believer. As verse 11 in the twelfth chapter of I Corinthians tells us, God gives these gifts just as He determines, not just because we want them. This can mean that some receive gifts for a lifetime while others may receive them only for the time they are needed in a specific situation. While the fruit of the Spirit is the abiding result of the transformation that the Holy Spirit works in the believer's personality, the gifts of the Spirit are given for the purpose of accomplishing some aspect of God's work.

Receipt of a gift from God's Holy Spirit brings responsibility with it. Peter urges us:

"Each one should use whatever gift he has received to serve others, faithfully administering God's grace in its various forms." (I Peter 4:10)

Jesus also instructs us when he says:

You are the salt of the earth. But if the salt loses its saltiness, how can it be made salty again? It is no longer good for anything, except to be thrown out and trampled by men. You are the light of the world. A city on a hill cannot be hidden. Neither do people light a lamp and put it under a bowl. Instead they put it on its stand, and it gives light to everyone in the house. In the same way let your light shine before men, that they may see your good deeds and praise your Father in heaven.

MATTHEW 5:13–16

If we receive a gift from the Holy Spirit, we must not keep it to ourselves as merely some kind of badge of honor or a sign that says we are special. We must use the gift, develop it, and encourage it to grow in service to God and mankind.

Twice Paul urges us to eagerly seek spiritual gifts; in Chapter 12:31, and in Chapter 14:1 of I Corinthians. But it is very clear from Scripture that we are not to seek gifts as a sign that we are being honored by God in a special way or as an indication that we are somehow special. We should seek the gifts as abilities that will help us better honor and serve the Lord. The gifts are not given to glorify us, but Him. Those who receive them are those who are ready to march forward wearing the armor of God.

The issue for us is not whether or not God will send us a gift. The question for us is whether or not we are ready to receive a gift or gifts. This is not a question to be taken lightly. There is much more involved than merely saying yes. The task that God has for you or me might totally disrupt the plans we have for ourselves. If I accept the gift of wisdom or knowledge and am called to teach, I may have to give up a very rewarding career as an attorney or a physician. I may have to sell my wonderful home and move into an inexpensive apartment. I may have to leave my home town and take my gift to some part of the world I've never even heard of. Are you ready to be used? Am I ready to be used? There would seem to be little point in giving us a gift which is merely a sign of what wonderful Christians we are, if we are not ready to apply the gift to the tasks at hand.

But do we have a choice? Does God let us choose? Can we say no? This is a very difficult question, and the best answer may be, "It depends." Just recently, in a sermon, Charles Stanley, pastor of the First Baptist Church of Atlanta, asked if Paul, then Saul, could have said "no" to God. Think about that. If any man ever had earthly reasons to say "no," it was Paul. His whole life up to that point had been aimed at the destruction of Christianity. All of his training, his social contacts, and his own zeal pointed him away from Jesus. Yet we have no indication that he hesitated or resisted the calling at all. Could he have said "no"?

It appears that only God can really answer that question. What we know for certain is that God's plan will be carried out. Whether it is Paul or someone else who is the instrument of his work may not be crucial. So, in most instances, it would seem that we have a choice. We can say "no" and God will find a willing channel somewhere else while we suffer the consequences of turning God down. Or we can say "yes" and bear the responsibilities that go with the task. Neither choice seems to be the easy way. However, if you accept the task, you can do so with the assurance that God will send you the gifts you need to carry out His work.

If, however, it is God's plan that a particular individual—you, me, or Paul—has already been chosen for the job, I doubt that we can refuse.

Seek the fruit of the Spirit, but you need not yearn for the gifts. They will come to you as God wishes and according to His need. Be eager to receive these gifts and to carry out God's work, but never seek these gifts as a sign that you are favored over those who have not received them.

We have seen that the gifts of the Holy Spirit are to be used to do God's work, to glorify Him. Those who are truly gifted use their gifts in love. They are not prideful and arrogant; they do not boast or make a great public display of their special talent. They do not flaunt their gift as a special sign. They know that their gift is not their own but is God acting through them. They simply go through their lives, quietly using the talent that God has placed in their trust to carry out the two great commandments:

> Hearing that Jesus had silenced the Sadducees, the Pharisees got together. One of them, an expert in the law, tested him with this question. "Teacher, which is the greatest commandment in the law?" Jesus replied, "Love the Lord your God with all your heart and with all your soul and with all your mind. This is the first and greatest commandment. And the second is like it: Love your neighbor as yourself. All the Law and the Prophets hang on these two commandments."
>
> MATTHEW 22:34–40

When we see the gifts are being used to carry out these commandments, we can know that they are truly gifts from God. Gifts used for any other reasons or in any other spirit are not genuine, they do not come from God, and they are to be avoided.

So, if we receive a gift from the Holy Spirit, we must not keep it to ourselves. We must use the gift, develop it, and encourage it to grow in service to God and mankind.

If our gifts are of the Spirit, we will not use them to seek fame, power, and money. This is not to say that material rewards will not be achieved. They very well may be. However, worldly reward is not the goal of those whose gifts are from God. The gifts of the Spirit cause us to want to do the best we can, to use our gifts in God's service in the best way possible.

The challenge is not for fame, power, or money, but to glorify God by using what He has given us to meet the challenges of His commandments.

Those whose gifts are not of the Spirit are more likely to see their gift as a steppingstone to fame and fortune. The gift itself is not appreciated nor is there a feeling of responsibility to use the gift for the well-being of others. There is a belief that the gift makes its recipient a special person, one more important than others, one who is entitled to being treated in a most favorable way by others. On the other hand, those whose gifts come from the Spirit see the importance of the task to be done and their responsibility in carrying it out. The manner in which the gift is used communicates a sense that God is the originator and the person is only a channel through whom God flows. There is a wonderful gospel hymn that expresses this relationship. The singer asks God to "Love Through Me."

We can ask God to let us take His gift of love to those who need it. We can use our finances through programs like Operation Smile so the gift of healing can be given to needy children. Through each of us the life of a lonely and homeless person can be changed, and in our business we can take the extra step to insure that we are giving value for our customers' dollars. I could pray that my teaching would reveal God to my students. Whatever your gift may be, use it to glorify God who is the source of all things. His gifts are precious. Always remember that and use them accordingly.

SOME QUESTIONS FOR THOUGHT AND DISCUSSION

1. Do you know people who possess one or more of the gifts of the Spirit listed by Paul. How did they use their gifts?

2. Are there people today with the gift of miraculous powers? If so, how do they use their gift?

3. The gift of "speaking in different kinds of tongues" is perhaps the most controversial of all the gifts listed by Paul. How do you feel about the author's discussion of this gift?

4. Do you believe that all Christians are given gifts of the Spirit?

5. Should we seek the gifts of the Spirit or wait for God to endow them upon us when we need them to carry out His work?

CHAPTER V

The Devil Lets You Do Good ... So You Won't Do Better

For the love of money is a root of all kinds of evil.
Some people, eager for money, have wandered from
the faith and pierced themselves with many griefs.
1 TIMOTHY 6:10

How does Satan work? What are the signs in our lives that Satan is in control, that he is having his way with us? Some would claim that everything that is tragic is caused by Satan. But it always seemed to me that the extent to which we experienced life's hard times or good times had little to do with our

belief in God or our commitment to Jesus. In fact, it appeared that there may even be a reverse or negative relationship. Those who are least spiritual often seem to get on best with life. Why should that be?

I first heard the sentence, "The devil lets you do good...so you won't do better," in a gospel song sung by a group called The Joys. When I heard it I was struck by just how profound that statement is. It occurred to me then that Satan has no tool more powerful than worldly success to distract us from God. Satan even tried this on Jesus when he tempted Him early in His ministry with worldly promises of food and power.

Satan's purpose is always to separate us from God and keep us separated. Anything he can do to accomplish that goal will be tried. He began his dirty work in the Garden of Eden when he persuaded Adam and Eve to disobey God. He put a barrier between them and God and in so doing introduced sin into the world. From that point on we have lived in a condition of sin and Satan loves it. In our natural state we are just where he wants us. Even with God's spirit within us, we are so caught up in matters of the world that God is often forgotten. Our lives are completely in the world.

> No one can serve two masters. Either he will hate the one and love the other, or he will be devoted to the one and despise the other. You cannot serve both God and money.
> MATTHEW 6:24

It can't be much clearer than that! If we love the world, if we are controlled by worldly desires, we cannot be fully committed to God. If we love God, we will not be controlled by worldly things. Which situation do you think Satan prefers?

In most cases, the devil has a pretty easy time of it. You see, the real world is not all that bad. There is a great deal in that world that pleases our bodies and even our souls. The body and the soul are part of the real world and are controlled by the natural laws that govern the world. The world is filled with much that we can enjoy. There is wealth, music, art, power, status, good food, and sexual pleasure. As long as striving to reach these goals comes first in our lives, we are serving the world. We are putting God in second place or giving Him no place at all in our lives.

Let's look at that passage from I Timothy again:

> For the love of money is a root of all kinds of evil. Some people, eager for money, have wandered from the faith and pierced themselves with many griefs.
>
> I TIMOTHY 6:10

This helps us understand the problem of the rich man:

> Then Jesus said to his disciples, "I tell you the truth, it is hard for a rich man to enter the kingdom of heaven. Again I tell you, it

is easier for a camel to go through the eye
of a needle than for a rich man to enter the
kingdom of God."

MATTHEW 19:23–24

The problem is not riches, power, fame, or physical pleasures. The problem is the love of these things,
a kind of love that binds us to the world. As long as
striving to reach these goals comes first in our lives,
we are serving the world. We are putting God after
these things.

In which direction are our souls focused, yours
and mine? Let's give ourselves a little test to see if we
can find out. You don't have to tell anyone else how
you answer these questions, but you do have to be
honest with yourself. (After all, God already knows
the answers.)

There are times when I don't go to church
because I want to sleep in, the weather is bad,
or I'd rather go to the beach or play golf. [Put
in your own leisure time favorite activity]

Yes____No____

When others want me to do things that I
am not comfortable doing, I usually go along
because I don't want to be different,

Yes____ No____

I have avoided helping someone in
need because it would have been
inconvenient for me to help.

Yes____No____

In order to please others, I have, at times,
failed to take a stand on matters of faith.

Yes____No____

I am attracted to people who are wealthy,
powerful, and famous and I wish I could be
like them.

Yes____No____

I give my time and money to God's work to
the extent that it is convenient.

Yes____No____

I seldom think about God unless things
are going badly.

Yes____No____

You get the point. Most of us who are being honest would have to admit to answering yes to some to
these questions. That is the natural way. That is the

way of the real world. It is so easy to be part of the crowd, to go for the gusto, to strive for material gain and to try to limit God to some convenient corner of our lives.

And you know what? If we play the world's game cleverly and somehow avoid the pitfalls and tragedies that are also a part of nature, we can achieve wealth, popularity, fame, and power. These things are there for the taking. Who needs God? The good life is already ours.

If you are on the worldly path, there is one thing you can be sure of. Satan will leave you alone! That's right. Set your sights on the world and the things of the world and you won't be bothered by Satan—because you are already his. So long as your eyes are focused on the things of the world, you are not focused on God, and that's exactly what Satan wants. It is only when you put God at the center of your life, when He comes first, that Satan will interfere and try to turn you away from God.

Some of us try to blame all of our troubles on Satan. There may be times when Satan does put barriers in our way, but I believe that most of the time our problems are not the work of Satan. Problems are more likely to simply be the result of being in the real world. As we have already seen, God's real world contains both riches and poverty, health and illness, joy and despair. All people are subject to all of the laws that govern nature. So long as a person stays on the side of riches, health, and joy, there may be little need for God. However, when our lot in life includes poverty, illness, and despair, we might find ourselves seeking God, turning to Him. Satan doesn't want that. The devil isn't happy to see church membership increasing in hard times. He's not pleased to see faith strengthened under political systems that try to stamp out religion and destroy our belief in God. The spiritual explosion now going on in Eastern Europe illustrates very clearly why Satan wants us to have it easy, to enjoy the "good life." Misfortune often turns us to God, not away from Him.

The devil knows that if we honestly seek God, we will find Him. And if we find Him, then we'll realize that there truly is something better than just the riches and power that come from the world. He doesn't want that to happen.

Let's suppose we're sailing along, doing well, and feeling good. Life is just fine. We're being good and doing good.

Then it happens! There is an accident, or a lost job, or the stock market crashes. Misfortune strikes.

If God has not been a part of your life and, even in times of distress, you do not turn to Him, the laws of nature will control your situation. If you are injured or sick, you will heal according to the healing properties of your body and any boost that medical science may give. If your problem is economic, the solution will be controlled by the economy. Satan isn't involved. God is not involved because you have chosen to keep Him out. Satan is happy.

Perhaps God has been a part of your life, but only in a casual way. You do some God work like Bible reading and church going but you really call on Him only when you're in trouble and this is one of those times. Satan will show up. He'll whisper little notions like "If there was a God He wouldn't have let this happen." You've heard that line in connection with natural disasters. "How could a loving God allow so much death and destruction?" Satan doesn't have to cause the problems. Instead, he works on your soul. He influences your thoughts, feelings, and your will. And once he puts the "What's the use" hold on you, the game is over. You no longer look to God; you just give up and go along with whatever the wind blows your way. You will now probably give up the little bit of God work you used to do. Satan is happy.

There are many devoted Christians who love Jesus and sincerely believe they would follow Him anywhere. They give time and money to His work, and they give generously. They may teach or preach. Their lives are dedicated. They are very much like Jesus' own apostles. Remember what happened to them? When the chips were really down, Peter denied Him. Thomas doubted and so did some of the others. Even those closest to Jesus, those who knew Him best and loved Him most had their doubts and nearly turned away.

Can't you imagine some of their conversations?

"Jesus is crucified. He is dead."
"If He had really been who we thought He was, they wouldn't have been able to kill Him."
"What shall we do now?"
"Do we go back to fishing and tax collecting?"
"I'm so discouraged."
"He seemed so powerful."
"I really thought He was the Messiah. I must have been wrong."
"This just couldn't happen to a Messiah."
And so on…

Change those questions that the apostles may have been asking each other to fit your own misfortune, your own discouragement. Listen carefully and you will hear that it is Satan's voice speaking to you, still trying to pull you away, still trying to get you to give up on this Jesus, this God, and cast your lot with the real world. After all, isn't that where we belong? If you do stop following Jesus there will be no more need for doubts, no reason to deny, and no persecution. And Satan will be happy.

So far, we've made it pretty easy for Satan. He has had to do nothing in some cases. When we have turned to God, Satan has had to put a few thoughts into our minds, but that's usually not hard for him to do. He even had the apostles going his way for a time. When Satan takes control, we begin to see the world as the source of everything that is the good life. When that happens, Satan's job is done. We are separated from God.

What could be better? Why not just leave well enough alone? Is there really anything wrong with going after the world's blessings? Money, power, and success are things you can use to make you and your family more comfortable. If you can earn it, why shouldn't you have it?

These are honest and good questions, but when we ask them, we are revealing that we haven't learned what God's promises for us are. The fact is, God wants us to be prosperous and happy, too. He wants you and me to enjoy the blessings of this world's abundance. But He wants you to have so much more.

Satan wants you to succeed, not because he's such a good guy, but because he knows that if he can hook you on the good things of the world you might be content with that. After all, why not? If you can "make it" and be comfortable, do you really need anything more?

But there is more. The world can't see it because the "more" is from outside of the world. It is beyond nature. It comes from God.

Both God and Satan want us to do well, be happy, and prosper. So what's the difference? The difference is that Satan wants us to love the worldly gifts. God wants us to enjoy and appreciate the source from which they have come. While Satan tries to tempt us to turn from God by offering worldly pleasures, God wants us to have all of the good things of the world *plus* the benefits of a life centered on Him. Let's see what those benefits are.

First and foremost, God offers salvation. He promises that we will spend eternity with Him. This is a matter of choice, our choice. God is always there, holding out His arms, wanting us to come to Him. He has already chosen us. Now we must choose Him. By choosing Him, we insure that our spirits, in a perfected body, will remain forever in the presence of God. If, on the other hand, we elect to remain focused on the world, we insure that we will spend eternity apart from God.

By taking this one simple step, by truly believing in Jesus Christ as Lord and Savior, we insure salvation of our spirit. That's one-up for God's people over those who choose to turn away from God. That's a pretty big one-up. Eternity in heaven sounds a lot better than eternity in hell.

The benefits and joys of God-centering our lives are not limited to the grace-given gift of an eternity in heaven. That ought to be good enough, you say. But actually that's the final reward, the last step. God promises more than eternal salvation. He is here with us as we live in this world. His presence with us makes all the difference.

Unlike Satan who merely allows us to do well, God helps us do well. The theme is repeated over and over in Scripture. Luke tells the story about Simon Peter's fishing trip:

> When he had finished speaking, he said to Simon, "Put out into deep water, and let down the nets for a catch." Simon answered, "Master, we've worked hard all night and haven't caught anything. But because you say so, I will let down the nets." When they had done so, they caught such a large number of fish that their nets began to break. So they signaled their partners in the other boat to come and help them, and they came and filled both boats so full that they began to sink.
>
> LUKE 5:4–7

Being a Christian means more than material blessing. In fact, God's blessing may very well be in some form other than goods or money. He is a healer. Christians do get sick with illnesses of all kinds. Some of us are born with bodily deficiencies. Some of us are afflicted with disease. Sometimes we have accidents. These things are part of being in the real world. Christians and non-Christians alike are subject to these misfortunes.

Christians and non-Christians have a God-given gift of healing. Illness and injury are usually overcome by the natural actions of the body. Sometimes the natural healing powers are helped by medical science. Everyone has these gifts. It is also true that

God heals both Christians and non-Christians when such healings contribute to the fulfillment of God's plans. God may use anyone at anytime to accomplish His purposes. If healing a non-Christian results in the salvation of even one person, that healing may be caused to happen in a miraculous way by God. If we stop and think about it, many of those healed by Christ were not actually His followers. But by healing those people, Jesus gave us a powerful illustration of who He was, His love, and His power. And by these illustrations, many are led to salvation.

So there are healing gifts for everyone. But there are special gifts for Christians. Christians can do better. Christ healed the woman who had suffered bleeding for twelve years and then said:

"... *your faith has healed you." (Matthew 9:22)*

In restoring sight to two blind men He said:

"... *according to your faith will it be done to you."*
(Matthew 9:29)

In his great book, *Love, Medicine, and Miracles*, Dr. Bernie S. Siegel, a noted surgeon reports case after case in which the faith and prayer of the patient strengthened the healing process, often in cases considered medically hopeless.

Christians are also the beneficiaries of an unshakable sense of security:

"And the peace of God, which transcends all understanding, will guard your hearts and your minds in Christ Jesus."
(Philippians 4:7)

"Peace I leave with you; my peace I give you. I do not

give to you as the world gives. Do not let your hearts be troubled and do not be afraid." (John 14:27)

In the King James version, Philippians 4:7 reads, in part, "... *the peace of God, which passeth all understanding.*"

How can I describe a peace that "passeth all understanding?" I can't, because it is a sense of peace that cannot be adequately described in words. If you have experienced it, you know what it is. It does not have to be explained to you. If you have not experienced it, there is no way for you to know what it is like. Like love, marriage, and parenthood, God's peace cannot be explained, but once you've experienced it you need no further explanation.

Those who know this peace are not overwhelmed by stress. As Christians face the trials of life, they carry with them a mighty weapon against the pressures caused by life's problems.

I am reminded again of Romans 8:28, *"And we know that in all things God works for the good of those who love him, who have been called according to his purpose."*

What a powerful statement! This goes beyond faith in Jesus Christ as Savior and beyond the power of prayer. Romans 8:28 is a promise of assurance that God has everything under control, including everything that happens to us, if we have been called according to His purposes.

On January 25, 1992, Nancy, my wife, was stricken at work with a serious weakness in her legs and an overwhelming feeling of fatigue. By the next day, a Sunday, the condition had worsened to the point that we had to get to an urgent care medical facility. She could scarcely walk and her condition was getting more serious by the hour. As we sat in the waiting room she said,

"Honey, whatever this is and whatever happens, I'm prepared. I'm not afraid. I know God is with me and I am ready for whatever He has planned for me. Right now I am claiming Romans 8:28."

She truly meant it. In a matter of a few hours she had become completely paralyzed from the waist down by a mysterious disorder known as Guillain-Barre Syndrome, which saps virtually all of the strength from the muscles it attacks. She was hospitalized for eleven days undergoing every medical test you can imagine. She was closely watched for any signs of the disease moving upward into the area of her heart and lungs where it would become a life-threatening problem. Fortunately, this did not happen. The disease only affected her legs, but for a week we could not be sure. During all of this, she remained serene, at peace. Friends would ask if she was afraid and were astounded to learn that she was not. She experienced the "peace that passeth all understanding." There was no fear because she knew that the promise of Romans 8:28 was true. Her assurance allowed her to minister to visitors who were amazed at her strength. She was happy to tell them where that kind of strength comes from.

LET'S SUMMARIZE.

Christians live in the real world and are subject to all of the good and bad things that happen in that world. They enjoy all of the good things that world has to offer. They may also suffer from the misfortunes that are part of the real world. In these ways, Christians and non-Christians have much in common. We all live in the same world and are subject to all of the laws of nature that control that world.

Both Christians and non-Christians may be prosperous. Both may enjoy an abundance of the world's blessings—wealth, power, status, and fame. Satan wants that. As long as we center our lives on worldly goals, we won't be centering our lives on Jesus. Our backs will be turned on God. God also wants us to prosper and enjoy the abundance of His creation. But instead of wanting us addicted to the world, God wants us to be His first, then He will shower us with His blessings.

All people are part of God's plan. He may use anyone to fulfill His purposes. Non-Christians may be healed if this furthers God's work. Christians may suffer if this is part of His plan.

In many ways Christians are just like everyone else. How are we different?

1. We will spend eternity in Heaven with the Father.

2. We have the healing power of faith, healing of both body and soul.

3. We have the power of prayer and through this we know God's presence. We experience answer to prayer in very direct and specific ways. We pray for others and we know these prayers work. And all of this according to God's plans.

4. We know the "peace that passeth all understanding." We know the assurance that comes from knowing that God is the source of all things and He is always in control.

Christians are different. "The devil lets you do good, so you won't do better."

SOME QUESTIONS FOR THOUGHT AND DISCUSSION

1. Describe what Satan means to you?

2. How does Satan work? Does he really allow us to be successful at times?

3. How has Satan influenced your life? What are some specific ways he has affected you?

4. Is Satan's tactic of separating us from God by giving us success effective? How can you prevent this from happening in your own life?

5. Do you have "the peace that passes all understanding?" How does this work in your life?

CHAPTER VI

Where is God Today?

The Lord reigns, he is robed in majesty; the Lord is robed in majesty and is armed with strength. The world is firmly established; it cannot be moved. Your throne was established long ago; you are from all eternity.
PSALM 93: 1–2

A few years ago we heard a great deal about God's death. The phrase, "God is Dead," was bandied about and even showed up on the cover of a national magazine. As we look at conditions in the world today, we might find it easy to reach that same sort of conclusion. From the looks of things all around the world, it may well appear that God is dead. Tragedy is everywhere. As I write there is strife in Iraq and throughout the Middle East. Those who were fellow countrymen are now at war with each other. North Korea and Iran are rattling nuclear sabers. There is famine and anarchy in many regions of Africa. Thugs, many of whom are scarcely out of childhood themselves, stand in the way of the delivery of food and other forms of help to dying children. A few years ago in Waco, Texas, many people, including children, died in a raging fire following a confrontation with government agents. They were members of a cult that claimed to be Christian. The world has experienced many natural disasters. Recently our mid-western states were devastated by the worst flooding on record and the mid-Atlantic states went through the driest month of July ever recorded. A tsunami obliterated a section of Indonesia and a hurricane devastated New Orleans and a large section of our Gulf States. We are told that within a few years much of our coastline will be inundated by rising water levels in our oceans. Pick any period of history and you can find all kinds of natural disasters and tragedies.

The victims are not just the bad guys. Children die, churches are swept away by hurricanes, fires, and floods. Christians and non-Christians alike suffer. Some people ask, "Where is God? Perhaps He is dead." To those who would ask such questions it sometimes seems that He is either dead or has abandoned us. It is certainly a problem that I have wrestled with for many years.

I have tried to answer this dilemma with the

notion that those who are hurt by acts of God are those who have sinned, who have turned their backs on Him and, therefore, deserve to be punished. But that answer won't do. When we see that many babies are afflicted with severe birth defects and diseases and we realize that Jesus Himself suffered a most painful, tragic and humiliating death, we must set aside the idea that tragedy is simply the result of being sinful.

Or look at it another way. Being sinless doesn't always protect us from the perils of living. It's especially important that we recognize this. There are those who claim to be teachers of the Gospel who would have us believe that if we are saved we are also protected from the perils and hardships in this life. Haven't you heard them? They tell us that God will solve every problem if we just ask. It also helps if you send them money or buy their trinkets. (Didn't Jesus cleanse the temple of these fellows?) They claim that if we are sick, God will heal us if we just ask Him. Or if we need money, we need only ask for it. We are led to believe that God protects those who love Him from the perils of living.

Of course, we know that God heals us, sometimes. He does provide money, sometimes. He does take us from harm's way, sometimes. And these blessings don't seem to be closely related to how good we are or how much we ask. Jesus was infinitely good, and He asked to be relieved of the burden of execution.

He was sinless. He knew how to pray to His Father. He asked, but He was crucified anyway.

Is the point made? Are the tragedies we experience in this life due only to sin, or is there more to it than that?

Maybe all of our problems are caused by Satan. What is his role in this world? Is he the master troublemaker? Doesn't it make sense to blame Satan for all of our difficulties? Can't we just say that God is good and that all good things come from Him, and Satan is evil and all bad things come from him? If that were true, we could all just line up behind God and He would protect us. But it isn't that simple. Again, we are reminded of Jesus and His suffering. We have no basis for believing that Satan caused the events surrounding Jesus' death. Perhaps he was there, dancing for joy. But I suspect it is more likely that Satan knew that the crucifixion and what would follow were not a victory for him, but a mortal defeat.

I believe it would be more accurate to say that all things come from God; those that we judge to be good and those that we judge to be bad. After all, He made it all. We have no evidence that Satan made anything. And as we have already noted, after God made it, He declared it good. His creation includes both the soft rain and the hurricane. It includes the warmth of the sun at the beach in the summertime and the sometimes fatal heat from the sun in the desert. Can we give God credit for the rain and sunshine only when we experience these things in a pleasant way and not also acknowledge that the hot sun and the storm are also His?

So let's come back to the question with which we started. Where is God in the midst of all of this tragedy? Be assured that He is here, and He is still in control. But where is He? Where can we see His work and feel His hand? To answer these questions we must look at how God provides us with opportunities to grow in times of distress, how He must sometimes punish us, and how God may view certain events that we see as tragedies.

We all know that if we lived in a world that contained no rough spots, we would not be able to appreciate the good times. Those of us who sat in the long gas lines of 1974 learned to appreciate, probably for the first time in our lives, the normally ready availability of gasoline. Not since World War II had there been limits placed on the purchase of such items. Because gasoline had always been so easy to obtain, we took the supplier for granted. But when supplies were not so easy to get, we began to realize how important the supplier was. Perhaps God placed us in a world of ups and downs so we would better appreciate the Source.

But we must look deeper than that. Maybe God places some barriers in our pathway to help us grow. That is the theme of a wonderful gospel song, "Lord, Please Don't Move That Mountain," and of this poem written by H. L. Marshall in *Aim for a Star:*

Against the frame of my heart I stood my
soul, its height I marked.
So small it was, so very small, I thought if
God could see it all. .
He'd understand it could not bear much
suffering, or pain, or care.
But though I knew that in God's eyes I must
appear of minute size;
Deaf to my pleas for leniency, He heaped
great burdens upon me;
And my poor soul was forced to bear what
seemed so much more than its share.
But, though it flinched and flinched anew,
somehow, (God must have known) it grew.
Each burden brought new strength, new
height.
I often think how well it might be small and
weak and helpless still.
If God had yielded to my will.

God knows that in order to grow we must sometimes struggle. A muscle is strengthened when we
work it. In order for our beliefs to make any difference in our lives we must exercise them. We are all
inspired by stories of people whose faith has grown
during times of stress and struggle. How much would
a student learn if the teacher presented no problems
to be solved? Don't we do a great deal of learning
in school because we know we will be tested? The
teacher who gives us a test is not being mean (though

we may think so at the time). Neither is God being mean when He confronts us with living tests.

Keep in mind that these challenges we find in our path are part of the design of the world. God doesn't have to go out of His way to make up a special task for us. They are already there. What He wants us to learn is that without Him we will be overwhelmed, but with His help we can handle any problem that comes along. This is how we grow spiritually, and that's the only thing that really matters. God wants us to know that He is always available, He is always at the center of our lives, and He is our resource for all things, including the strength and skill needed to climb any mountain we encounter. God is there in times of trouble to help us grow closer to Him.

There are times when loving parents must punish their children. There are some behaviors that come naturally to inquisitive, active children that are dangerous and sometimes life-threatening. Children will play in the medicine chest or with the cleaning supplies under the sink. Very young children will try out new items in their world by tasting and chewing them. Children playing in the yard will dart into the street without thinking. Horseplay on a boat or near a swimming pool is a natural thing for children to do, but it is potentially fatal. To stop these things from happening, we have to use some form of punishment. (To you who might feel that any form of punishment is wrong, I recommend that you research the question of how to eliminate random levels of potentially harmful behaviors.) I am not saying we must be abusive. Mild punishment can be effective if it is consistent and delivered promptly. The child must learn that there is a definite relationship between the behavior and the consequences of that behavior.

Is it then strange and unexpected that God would punish us for certain actions? If we engage in behaviors that are destructive to ourselves as well as others, that take us away from Him instead of drawing us closer, mustn't He, as a loving parent, take steps to turn us around, including steps that seem to be punishing? It is the loving thing to do.

The Bible gives us so many accounts of God's use of punishment. He punished Adam and Eve by removing them from the Garden of Eden. He punished the whole world except for Noah's family and the animals with a flood. He refused to allow the original band of Israelites who fled from Egypt to enter the Promised Land, and this even included Moses. The apostles were punished in various ways. Even Paul suffered his "thorn in the flesh" along with numerous beatings and imprisonment.

What was gained from all of that? In some cases, we know how the individuals who were punished felt. Think of how Peter suffered after denying Christ and what then happened to him. Study the life of Paul and you will hear him giving thanks for this "thorn" that helped to keep him humble and aware that the source of his strength was not his own body but the Lord.

But there is more to it than that. Does knowing from the examples given to us in Scripture that God surely disciplines His children help us in any way? I believe that it does. I know that when things aren't going as I would like in my own life, I look closely at my relationship with God and at my own behavior. I am certain that if I am pulling away from God or doing things that are out of His will, He will punish me. I am also certain that the punishment He inflicts on me may be a lesson to others just as the accounts we find in the Scripture are lessons to us all.

There is a big problem here. Maybe you've already noticed it. Do you want to ask how someone who has been killed in a natural disaster can possibly learn from his experience? Or how about all of those people killed in the great flood? Only Noah and his family were saved. These questions lead us to the next point.

We know that God cares about human events. Jesus was God Incarnate, God in the flesh for a brief moment in history. And during that time, He experienced sadness and He wept over some of the things people around Him experienced. We know He was sensitive to human discomfort because He fed the hungry multitudes. He healed the sick and raised the dead. He comforted the depressed. From the life of Jesus we know that God cares and that He feels the pain we feel. In fact, He is the one who created in us the capacity to experience such feelings.

But if we die, does God hurt as we do? Or is

physical death a step toward returning home and, therefore, a time for rejoicing? Don't the jazz musicians in New Orleans have it right when their music at a funeral first mourns the loss of a friend or loved one, but then rejoices in the spiritual triumph which this event represents?

As we look at human events, including those that seem so tragic, we are again reminded of the promise of Romans 8:28. This verse reminds us that God is much bigger, much wiser, much more magnificent than we can ever comprehend. And yet we are forever trying to reduce Him to our size, to understand His works in the limited human terms that we can understand. Just the other day I heard someone make the claim that we believe in God so long as He agrees with us. I have also heard it said that we create God in our own image instead of the other way around. God is too big for that kind of thinking.

We must never try to reduce God to our level. He is so much greater, so much grander than we are that we can never fully comprehend His magnificence. We use big words like omnipotent, omnipresent, and omniscient to try to express this grandeur that is God, but we can never truly grasp His greatness. But, you see, we don't really need to understand it. It is simply a matter of faith that we accept. Know that God is loving, and great, and wise, and powerful and caring far beyond our ability to know and understand. And then, just let it go at that. Accept that as a matter of faith and don't try to analyze it.

And don't try to "explain" God because you can't do it. Our minds simply cannot grasp God in any sure and certain way. To assume that you can know Him fully is putting yourself right up there with Him and I don't think you or I belong there.

We can never know Him completely. We can learn about God from the Bible, but He is much bigger than any book. What is in the Bible is true, but that is not all there is to God. We can learn of God through our personal experiences, but He is bigger than that. We can learn from the experiences of others and from the world God created for us. But He is more than all of those things combined. We might come to know some of His features, but we must remember that those features are only parts and not the whole of God.

I am reminded of the story of the blind men who were trying to determine what an elephant is by touching him. One felt his trunk and described the elephant accordingly. Another felt his tusks, another a leg, and yet another the tail. Each man could accurately describe the part of the elephant he had experienced, but none could describe the whole elephant.

We are much like the blind men when it comes to knowing God or knowing why He allows certain things to happen. We each know Him in our own way and what we know is correct, but none of us, no human being, can see the whole picture.

We can say that God is everywhere and in everything. He is all knowing and all caring. He is all powerful. Nothing happens that He is not a part of. He made nature and He made all of the rules that govern it. When necessary, we know He can modify the rules, but He doesn't have to do that except in rare cases because He has already made the rules that control everything. And the rules He made, like all of creation, are good. If we must climb mountains, endure punishment, or face tragedy, we do so knowing that He is with us and in control of everything at all times. The fact that you and I can't understand why He does things as He does is beside the point. We don't need to understand. We just need to walk in faith. God is not dead.

SOME QUESTIONS FOR THOUGHT AND DISCUSSION

1. What caused many people to claim that God is dead? Is He?

2. The author seems to believe that Christians are just as susceptible to tragedy as others are. Is that how you interpreted what he wrote? How do you feel about this issue?

3. What role do you think Satan plays in the tragedies of life?

4. Why in your opinion, does God allow those who love and follow Him to suffer or die in tragic ways?

5. What is your reaction to the following quotation from the author? "To assume that you can know Him (God) fully is putting yourself right up there with Him and I don't think you or I belong there."

CHAPTER VII

The Bible–A Guidebook for Living

*All Scripture is God-breathed and is use-
ful for teaching, rebuking, correcting and training in righteousness, so that the man of God may
be thoroughly equipped for every good work.*
2 TIMOTHY 3:16–17

What are we to make of this wonderful book we call
the Bible? It continues to be the best-selling book in
history, is in more homes, and is read by more people
than any other book ever written—by far. When the
printing press was invented, the Bible was the first
book printed. It has been translated into virtually all

written languages, and it has been the reason that many spoken languages have been put into written form. The Bible is available to more people than any other book or document in print.

I could go on recording the accomplishments achieved by the Bible, which prove how powerful its influence has been on the lives of us all, but that isn't really necessary. We are all familiar with the Bible's record.

What we do need to consider, however, is just how the Bible has earned a place of such influence and prominence in our lives. What is it about these writings that has maintained them in a position of reverence and respect that has persisted through so many centuries?

Before answering that question, let us consider the viewpoint that the Bible is a grand hoax, a great scheme concocted by creative and clever writers from the ancient world designed to delude readers into believing a fairy tale. There are people who hold such a belief. I have worked with some of them.

There are others among my ex-colleagues who would argue that the Bible is the result of a grand delusion. The writers of the Bible are not viewed as creative geniuses who have purposefully attempted to deceive their readers, but as misguided individuals who were attempting to get their readers to accept a reality that existed only in the writers' minds, their imaginations.

These critics will usually attempt to focus attention on the Bible's records of miraculous events and claim that such things never happened because no tangible evidence can be produced to "prove" the stories. For example, the story of Noah and the ark is considered to be untrue because no one has found the ark. By the same token, the story of Adam and Eve is not believed because we haven't located the Garden of Eden. Supposed contradictions in the Bible are also pointed to as indications that the Bible is not true. The account of the creation of man and woman, Adam and Eve, in the first chapter of Genesis is not exactly the same as the account given in the second chapter of the same book. There definitely seems to be a contradiction.

Whether the critic claims purposeful trickery, or delusion on the part of the writers, or emphasizes the impossibility of miracles, or asserts that contradictions in the Bible text make it an untrue and unreliable document, the answer to the criticism is the same. The answer to the critics is best given in the form of a question:

Could a false statement, whether false by design or false by delusion, have achieved and maintained the status and influence enjoyed by the Bible through so many centuries?

The idea that mankind could be fooled so completely and for so long a time seems even further removed from reality than some of the events recorded in the Bible seem to its critics.

Actually, the Bible needs no defense. Its record

stands for itself. Perhaps the skeptics would like to put their records on the line. Shall we recognize even one of them in a few hundred years? Look back in time and name the works of one critic from the past who is well-known or whose works have made the slightest dent in the influence of the Bible.

If the Bible is more than fiction, more than a fairy tale, then what is it? What has kept it in a very special position of prominence for so many years?

The answer to that question goes deeply into the bond that connects God and man. We know that there is within us a spirit, a spirit that makes us children of God, made in His image. It is the spirit that Paul speaks of in the first chapter of Romans, the spirit which allows us to sense God's presence.

When we read the Bible, we feel God there in the words and in the inspiration of those who wrote the words. We relate to that presence and that power in a way that is different from our bond to any other writing. We may appreciate and be deeply moved by the literary genius of a Shakespeare or the music of a Mozart or Beethoven, but these works, as magnificent as they truly are, pale before the power of the Bible. It is through the Bible that we have our closest, regular contact with God. We experience God in a most powerful way in some of the events of our lives, but these are occasional events. We may feel God's presence in a very close way when they occur, but it is through the Bible that God speaks to us every time we meet Him there. Spirit meets spirit. And it is through the spirit that we sense and recognize the presence of God. No work of man's genius in literature, art, or music contains that spirit in the way it is found in the Bible, and it is for that reason the Bible has had an influence on the world far beyond that of any other work.

We feel this special quality of the Bible and the way it links us to God when we face the question of getting rid of one. Perhaps we have acquired several new Bibles and truly do not need to keep an older copy. Or maybe our Bible is in such a tattered state that it is hardly usable. When this happens, can you throw your Bible away as easily as you can some other book? Most people can't, and the reason is that spiritual quality that bonds us to God through the Bible and makes it a truly holy book. The Bible is a meeting ground for God's spirit and the spirit of God within us and we cherish that in a very special way.

The spirit through which we sense God's presence in the Bible is not the Holy Spirit. The spirit makes us aware, the Holy Spirit enables us to understand and act on God's word in a most profound way. In my own personal experience, before I invited the Holy Spirit into my life, I read the Bible a great deal but without much effect on my life. After making the Holy Spirit a partner, the Bible came alive in new and special ways which I described in an earlier chapter.

Those who accept the Bible as God's word all agree that it is an inspired document. However, there is a great deal of disagreement among believers regarding the way in which the writers of the Bible were inspired.

Before getting into the question of just what "inspiration" means, let's consider the matter of how authentic the documents we have are. The original writings of the books that make up our Bible, both Old and New Testament, were done in Greek, Hebrew, and Aramaic. From time to time, as older manuscripts are discovered, we have an opportunity to check the accuracy of more recent versions. Over and over again, the findings are the same. There have been virtually no changes in these documents from the earliest known versions found to the most recent. The few changes which have been made and which have been identified tend to be minor and do not, in any important ways, change the basic message of the Scripture.

We must keep in mind that we probably have none of the original writings. What we have are copies which have been made from generation to generation by scholars from a culture that revered its religious heritage and dedicated itself to preserving that heritage. Nowhere else in antiquity can we find such careful and thorough devotion to scholarship as we find among those who preserved the Scriptures, both Old and New Testaments.

It seems reasonable to conclude that if the accuracy record is virtually perfect and unbroken for as far back as we can now trace it, that it is most probably equally reliable all the way back to the original manuscripts. With this assurance that we do have access to genuine copies of the first writings, we can begin to consider the question of inspiration.

When we refer to inspiration, we are referring to those writers who took pen in hand and recorded the messages they received from God. We are referring to those whose names we know, and to many others whose names are lost to us. In some way, God led them all to record His message for His people and they did so.

How were they inspired? There are those who would argue that the writers were basically channels for God's words, that He dictated His message by putting His words into their mouths, or their pens, to be more accurate. From this viewpoint, the writers were stenographers recording as God dictated. If this view is correct, the Bible is literally God's word, as He spoke it, word-for-word, from beginning to end.

Inspiration may be viewed in another way. Instead of dictating word-for-word, perhaps God has given certain writers both the need to express God's message to His people and the ability to do this in a very special way. This kind of inspiration goes far beyond a mere urge to write about one's experiences or views. Truly inspired writing catches the spirit of God in a way that makes it recognizable to the spirit within us, the readers.

Writing inspired in this way may take many forms. There may be history, poetry, music, drama, and even fiction. In our secular world we use all of these ways to communicate our heritage, our culture, and our understanding of other times and places. Isn't our view of the Old West or the Civil War a combination of these various forms of communication? History should be supported by as much evidence, such as documents and physical evidence, as we can obtain to verify the historical reports. But we don't require that the music or fiction, which may also tell us a great deal about some period in history, be limited to historically proven facts. Is the value of a book like *Gone With the Wind* dependent on finding a plantation named Tara and documents to prove that the O'Hara family actually lived there?

Is it possible that God has chosen to reveal Himself to us in these various ways in Scripture? He is there in history, but He is also there in song and in stories that tell us about Him in the form of parables and allegories. If this is true, then we will find that some parts of the Bible can be backed up with physical evidence, and the more we dig the more such evidence we are finding. But He can also reveal Himself in ways which we cannot verify physically, and the fact that verification is not possible, does not mean that the writing is not inspired or valuable to us.

I have chosen to believe that God has inspired those whose works make up the Bible to use all forms of communication available to them in communicating His truth, His revelation, to us. The truth that comes to us in poetry or parable is just as much a revelation of God as is the historical record. It really doesn't matter if every event mentioned in the Bible took place exactly as it is recorded. I don't feel the need to insist on scientific verification for each event. Neither do I believe we need to claim a miracle in each case in which we are unable to adequately document a report. I am satisfied, for example, that a writer was inspired by God to reveal a truth or truths about God through the story of the flood and the ark. If that story can be documented as historical, that is fine. But if it can't be documented, I am not troubled. The message is still the same and if the writer was inspired to write an allegory instead of history to communicate the message, I am satisfied. Quite honestly, there is enough verification of many of the writings already available to satisfy me that the historical record is essentially accurate. I find that the other writings, the non-historical forms, enrich and illuminate the historical record and add to the fullness of God's revelation of Himself to us.

For me, there is one exception to the notion that reports in Scripture might be believed as either historically true or as allegory or parable. I believe the accounts of the life, death, and resurrection of Jesus in the Gospels are true as stated.

I am aware that there are some who feel that the King James Version is the only true Bible. I respect their enthusiasm and commitment, but I do not share their point of view. It is my feeling that God's inspiration didn't cease in 1611 when the King James

Version of the Bible was compiled. God's inspiration has continued through the years, and has resulted in God revealing Himself over and over again in many ways, including the works of the many people who have created the various translations of the Bible which have been produced since the King James Bible was done. God speaks to us where we are and in ways which we can grasp. In my study, I often find it helpful to read the same portion of Scripture in several versions. Sometimes each translation provides a bit of insight I did not receive from the other versions. Consider the following examples:

I Peter 2:1–3 from the King James version:

> Wherefore laying aside all malice, and all guile, and hypocrisies, and envies, and all evil speakings, as newborn babes, desire the sincere milk of the word, that ye may grow thereby: if so be ye have tasted that the Lord is gracious.

I Peter 2:1–3 from the Living Bible:

> So get rid of your feelings of hatred. Don't just pretend to be good! Be done with dishonesty and jealousy and talking about others behind their backs. Now that you realize how kind the Lord has been to you, put away all evil, deception, envy, and fraud. Long to grow up into the fullness of your salvation; cry for this as a baby cries for his milk.

And the same passage from the New International Version:

> Therefore, rid yourselves of all malice and all deceit, hypocrisy, envy, and slander of every kind. Like newborn babies, crave pure spiritual milk, so that by it you may grow up in your salvation, now that you have tasted that the Lord is good.

On the first reading of the King James Version, I found it difficult to grasp the meaning of the passage. After reading the same verses in the other versions, I began to understand and could, in fact, return to the King James Version with a greater appreciation of its message. Each version seems to enrich the next and vice-versa. And, after all, it is God's message we are after, not the worship of a particular translation. We should use the version or combination of versions that best allows us to hear God speaking to us.

If the Bible is merely a hoax or the work of the imaginations of its writers, it is of no real consequence to us. We need not pay attention to its teaching, and we may either appreciate or ignore the beauty and power of its writings. We may accept or reject it part by part. The context in which verses of Scripture are found would be of no real importance since the value of the verse would be found in the cleverness with which it is expressed and our own creativeness in attaching the verse to some issue relating to our lives. The Bible, then, becomes a book of clever quotations that may be used or discarded according to the will of the reader.

However, if the Bible is what it claims to be—the inspired word of God, one of God's ways of revealing Himself to us—we must approach it and study it accordingly. We cannot separate out those portions of His word that displease us, leaving only the parts with which we agree. We cannot twist its meaning to bring His message into agreement with our own preconceived notions.

One overriding message running throughout the Scriptures is that we must love one another, care for our neighbors, and leave judgment to God. And yet there are those who call themselves Christians who clearly and blatantly reject, harass, and even attack those with whom they disagree and try to justify it by claiming to be God's agents. God's work must not be used in that way.

If the message of the Bible is inspired by God, whether it be in literal terms or through the talents of those chosen to write it, it must be taken seriously in its entirety. We must not believe on the one hand, that God inspired the writings that relate to how we should live our daily lives, but did not inspire those who wrote about salvation. We must not by-pass those portions of Scripture that admonish us for our disputes over doctrinal issues and focus only on those passages with which we agree. We cannot trust God to save us by His grace and then disregard the teachings that tell us to rely on Him in matters of vocation, personal relationships, family, or finances. The message of the Bible is all of one piece, it is all of God, and we must receive it and respond to it accordingly.

SOME QUESTIONS FOR THOUGHT AND DISCUSSION

1. What is it about the Bible that has sustained it through the centuries? Do you agree with the author's view or do you feel differently about this?

2. How do you feel about the various translations of the Bible that are available to us?

3. In what way do you believe the Bible is an "inspired" book?

4. React to the following statement taken from a newspaper article:

   "... the Bible's interpretation needs to change with the times."

5. Discuss the role of the Bible in the life of the Christian.

CHAPTER VIII

Prayer—Releasing the Power

And when you pray, do not be like the
hypocrites, for they love to pray standing
in the synagogues and on the street corners
to be seen by men. I tell you the truth, they
have received their reward in full. But when
you pray, go into your room, close the door
and pray to your Father, who is unseen. Then
your Father, who sees what is done in secret,
will reward you.

MATTHEW 6:5–6

When we read our Bible, God reveals Himself to
us. We meet Him there in the pages of that wonder-

ful book and receive the messages He has for us. But our most intimate and powerful association with Him comes when we meet Him in prayer. In these meetings we not only hear His words for us, we also express ourselves to Him. Prayer provides us with an opportunity for our most personal contact with the Father. It is, therefore, vital to our Christian experience that we learn to pray as God would want us to, and we learn that by going to Scripture to the greatest of all teachers, Jesus, Himself.

Jesus Teaches Us How to Pray

The Gospels contain a number of references to Jesus' teachings regarding prayer and His own prayer life. In the books of Matthew and Luke we learn of the Lord's Prayer, the prayer which Jesus taught. It was early in His ministry when this teaching was given. John the Baptist had been instructing his followers in prayer and those who were with Jesus asked Him to help them as John was helping his followers. Jesus answered them with these words recorded in the book of Matthew:

> This, then, is how you should pray: "Our Father in heaven, hallowed be your name, your kingdom come, your will be done on earth as it is in heaven. Give us today our daily bread. Forgive us our debts, as we also have forgiven

our debtors. And lead us not into temptation,
but deliver us from the evil one."

MATTHEW 6:9–13

Notice that Christ did not teach that the specific words of the prayer be recited. In fact, we have no record that He ever used this prayer Himself. He told His followers "how" to pray, not "what" to pray. This suggests that the Lord's Prayer is a guideline or a model rather than something to be repeated word for word. I don't believe this means we should never repeat the words He gave us, but it does mean that we are not limited to just these words. Our prayers should convey the meaning of the Lord's Prayer, not necessarily its actual words, and it should always come from the heart, not just the head. Mere repetition of the words is not praying.

As we should expect, there are many minor differences between the various versions of the Lord's Prayer that are available to us. Matthew and Luke offer slightly different wordings and there are differences between the translations. For example, the King James Version includes a familiar last line that is not in other well-known versions.

"... *For thine is the kingdom and the power and the glory, forever. Amen." (Matthew 6:13)*

In Luke, the word "sins" is used instead of "debts" and if we continue reading the account in Matthew in the King James Version we find the word "trespass" used in verses 15 and 16. The combination of terms such as "debts," "sins," and "trespasses" communicates more to us than any one of the terms would when used alone. We should not, therefore, be disturbed by the differences we find in the different versions. Instead, we may use the diversity to enrich our understanding of this teaching.

Let's look at the different parts of the Lord's Prayer:

OUR FATHER IN HEAVEN

It is clear from this statement that our prayers are to be directed to God the Father, not Jesus, not the Holy Spirit, not Mary or any of the saints. We pray to the Father, the Father in heaven, not an earthly father.

This teaching is basic to one of the fundamental beliefs of Protestantism. In the early years of the Christian Church, believers were taught that someone else had to do the praying or that prayers had to go through an intermediary in order to reach God. The believer was not "qualified" to go directly to the Father. Now we know better than that. Jesus, Himself, taught us that we can and, indeed, we should pray directly to God. We do not need a go-between to convey our prayers to the Father.

HALLOWED BE YOUR NAME

Each time we pray we should make it a point to praise God, to let Him know that we worship and adore Him and that we hold Him at the center of our lives. We recognize Him as the source of all things. *Webster's New Collegiate Dictionary*, 7th Edition, defines "hallowed," "1. to make holy or set apart for holy use. 2. to respect greatly, venerate."

We can forgive Webster for implying that we make God holy when we use the word hallowed when referring to Him or praying to Him. God is, of course, already holy. He does not need us to grant holiness to Him. Our prayer merely acknowledges this holiness and verifies our adoration and our trust in Him.

YOUR KINGDOM COME, YOUR WILL BE DONE

The world is in a terrible mess. It always seems to be that way. We are forever wishing that somehow God will wipe away all of the pain and tragedy and replace it with a world that offers us eternal bliss. But we have already seen, in previous chapters, that at least some of the tragedy we experience is a normal and natural part of the world God has created for us.

Whatever the case, when we pray that God's kingdom come, we cannot expect Him to change His design for the world. God is perfect, and He is forever unchanging. What we must pray for is a change in mankind's response to God, a change in our souls. It is in our souls that God can enter in. He has already promised that, and He is simply waiting for our call. So when we pray for His kingdom to come, what we must do is open ourselves up to Him. We must pray for ourselves, and for others, that God, by way of the Holy Spirit, will come into us and bring His kingdom, and bless us with the fruit of the Holy Spirit. We must let Him in. Then, at some later time, we will join Him in His heavenly kingdom.

Jesus also teaches us to pray that God's will be done; not ours, not society's but His will.

There are some who feel that when we pray and then ask that it be God's will rather than our own, we are showing a lack of faith. They argue that if we truly believed and were truly guided by the Holy Spirit, we would know God's will and always be in it. We wouldn't have to qualify our prayer by asking for His will.

This viewpoint fails to recognize that we are still human and, therefore, unable to fully know God's will. We still possess human frailties, limitations, and imperfections. Even Jesus, in the Garden of Gethsemane, asked to be relieved of the burden facing Him, but then added that it was the Father's will, not His, which was to be done. I believe the Lord's Prayer does teach us to ask that God's will be done when we pray.

GIVE US TODAY OUR DAILY BREAD

Notice that we are praying not just for ourselves, but also for others. We do not say, "Give me my daily bread." We pray for "us." And we pray for necessities, our daily bread, not for the extras, the luxuries we sometimes wish for. Actually, it is probably all right to pray for these things, but if we do so, we are going beyond the scope of what Jesus told us to pray for and the likelihood of response is small.

But we should pray for the things we truly need. God wants to sustain us so we may carry out the plan He has for our lives. Therefore, when we ask for our daily bread, we are asking for the sustenance, nurture, and health needed to be God's disciple. When we pray in this manner, we are assured that God will give to us, and those we pray for, what we need to carry out the tasks He has set before us, and that is what we must pray for. God is ready and willing, but we have to let Him know that we love Him, trust Him, and are ready to serve Him. We are His army of volunteers. When we pray for our daily bread we are telling God that we have made the choice to serve Him and that we are ready. He will not force us, but He will prepare us when we ask.

FORGIVE US OUR DEBTS AS WE FORGIVE OUR DEBTORS

We ask God to forgive us and He will. But there is a stipulation. We will be forgiven to the extent that we forgive others. Being forgiven depends on forgiving. The person who seeks to get even or get revenge or to punish those who are perceived as enemies cannot expect his or her debts to be forgiven until there is a change of heart.

Our inability to truly forgive others is a sure sign of a lack of faith. God promises us that He will judge, He will take care of those who need to be punished. When we hang on to our hostilities and ill-will towards others, we are saying that we do not truly trust God to carry out His word. Do we believe in God enough to let Him decide who needs to be punished and what that punishment shall be? Only when we can do that can we let go and forgive that person for whatever wrong we feel they have done to us.

Trusting God also allows us to forgive by helping us realize that God is in control of all things in the life of the believer. When things happen to us that may seem dreadful at the time, we often tend to look for someone to blame. If, however, we can realize that whatever happens to us is subject to the principle given us in Romans 8:28, we are less likely to blame others and more likely to look for God's will in our circumstances. I heard this eloquently expressed in a sermon about Joseph and his ability to forgive his brothers for threatening to kill him and eventually selling him into slavery in Egypt. Joseph was able to see his brothers as agents carrying out God's plan for his life.

Only after we have forgiven can we expect God to forgive us. So when we pray we must ask first that we may be able to forgive, so that, in turn, God can forgive us.

And don't forget that forgiving is unconditional, done with the kind of grace and mercy that God offers us.

LEAD US NOT INTO TEMPTATION, BUT DELIVER US FROM EVIL

The key phrase here is "deliver us from evil." Don't try to break this up into two separate thoughts. If we simply ask God not to lead us into temptation we are asking Him not to do something He would never do in the first place. God does not lead us into temptation. We do that quite well on our own. However, using this phrase serves to remind us of the presence of temptation and our weakness in trying to deal with it.

When we do give in to temptation and let those qualities of the old nature take control, we are courting evil. Remember Adam and Eve. They chose to make a deal with the serpent and man has never been the same since.

But God can deliver us from evil by sending us the Holy Spirit, which will empower us to cast aside the old nature and give us the strength to remove evil from our lives. This is what we are praying for when we ask God to deliver us from evil. We are asking for the power of the Holy Spirit and when we truly ask, we will receive it.

When we pray, our prayer should be directed to God the Father in a way that recognizes and praises Him for his holiness. We need to pray for God's intervention in our lives, the lives of others, and the affairs of the world. And we should ask God to provide us with whatever we need to do His bidding in our lives. We must ask for His forgiveness, but we do so recognizing that we must first forgive if God is to forgive us. And we should always pray that the Holy Spirit be with us to give us the strength we need to cope with the pitfalls, dangers, and evils we constantly face.

By His teaching and example, Jesus also taught us where to pray. It is abundantly clear that Jesus considered prayer to be a private matter. Over and over He reminds us to pray in private: *"But when you pray, go into your room, close the door and pray to your Father, who is unseen," (Matthew 6:6)*

We can see from Jesus' own behavior that He did not mean that we should literally go into a closed room. He withdrew from the crowd, even from His own disciples, when He prayed. But He didn't always go into a room. He went up on the mountain, or into the garden, or to another section of the boat, away from the others.

We have two references to times when Jesus spoke to His Father in public. This took place during the crucifixion and on one other occasion recorded in Matthew:

> At that time Jesus said, "I praise you, Father, Lord of heaven and earth, because you have hidden these things from the wise and learned, and revealed them to little children. Yes, Father, for this was your good pleasure."
>
> MATTHEW 11:25–26

This took place while Jesus was talking with a crowd about John the Baptist. But we have no record that He ever delivered a formal, extensive prayer during worship service or in public. Neither did His followers do that. A review of the New Testament produced no record of any of the apostles, including Paul, delivering public prayer. We find nothing about prayers of the type we regularly use in our worship services in which a minister or priest delivers what are sometimes rather lengthy discourses.

Even though there seems to be no New Testament authority for public prayer, it does have a place in our worship services. Jesus referred to the temple as a house of prayer and spoke of praying in the temple. He did speak rather strong words against the pompous, self-serving prayers of the Jewish leaders offered mainly to call attention to the person making the prayer. However, public prayers that help direct and enrich our private prayers do not seem to be discouraged by Jesus.

From His teaching and His life, Jesus encouraged prayer as an intimate relationship between each of us and God the Father. He prayed in that manner and He encourages us to do likewise.

Jesus not only taught us how to pray, He taught us when to pray. We are told to pray without ceasing, to be constantly in prayer. Does this mean that we should be reciting our prayers continuously? Such an interpretation seems rather doubtful. We do continue to live in a real world in which we have responsibilities to others as well as to God. The second great commandment, which tells us to love our neighbors, makes that very clear. There have been those who have withdrawn from society, and even from speaking aloud, to live lives in which all thoughts and actions focus directly on God. That hardly seems the way God expects most of us to live.

Being constantly in prayer means having God at the center of our lives, seeing Him as the source of all things, and being the one who is in control of all things. When confronted with a difficult situation, the prayerful person's first thoughts are of God and their lives reflect this attitude. His presence is seen in all things.

I am a bit insecure when writing about this for fear of suggesting to the reader that if we surround ourselves with religious ornaments, keep our radios tuned to Christian stations, and display our Bibles prominently throughout the house, these things will remind us to be prayerful, and this will satisfy the requirement to pray without ceasing. This is, however, focusing attention on the outward signs rather than the inner soul. And it is the soul which must be in prayer.

If we are in prayer without ceasing:

1. We appreciate that the source of all nurture; food, water, air, and life itself is God.

2. Praising God is a normal and natural thing to do and does not need to be prompted.

3. We automatically think about how God would have us handle a situation rather than experiencing God as a second thought or not at all.

4. Praying to God is a natural act occurring throughout the day rather than on a schedule.

These are the kinds of signs that let us know that we are constantly in prayer and God is always there at the focal point of our lives.

What happens when we pray? Why do we keep on praying? Psychology tells us that we continue to do something because it works. Our behavior is strengthened when it meets our need. Since people have been praying for at least as long as we have any records of human behavior, it is reasonable for us to conclude that we persist in praying because it brings results.

Most people pray. In a study of one hundred patients about to undergo heart surgery done at the University of Alabama School Of Nursing and the U. S. Air Force Nurse Corps, ninety-six of the patients reported that prayer had been a part of their preparation for surgery. Surveys consistently show that prayer is an important part of the lives of most Americans, and in spite of the controversy surrounding prayer in public places such as schools, there are still a number of situations in which prayer is offered as part of the proceedings. I believe the United States Congress still begins its sessions with prayer. We are a praying people.

What are the effects of prayer?

1. Prayer relieves stress.

2. Prayer changes things.

3. Prayer heals.

4. Prayer makes us receptive to God's will.

Let's look at each of these outcomes of prayer.

Prayer relieves stress

God has given us a wonderful gift that allows us to share our burdens with Him and with others. When we share our burdens we experience some relief from the stress caused by those burdens. When we talk with a friend about a problem in our lives, the very act of talking it out with someone who cares some-how makes the load seem lighter. This happens even if the person cannot actually help with solving the problem. The sharing itself makes a difference.

Just think of the even greater relief we will experience when we share our concerns with God. God is bigger and stronger than any problem we might have. He is waiting to be asked and when asked He will step in to help. We not only share when we talk it over with God, we get His involvement.

PRAYER CHANGES THINGS

One of the big stumbling blocks we face in turning our problems over to God is our unwillingness to also turn the solution over to Him. When we ask God to deal with a situation in a certain way, our way, we are not actually trusting Him. God's way is already determined. We are not going to change His mind, so once we invite Him in we must be prepared to accept His way of doing things. He may even turn things around and insist that we solve our own problem, but in that case, He will give us the tools we need to do the job.

I have asked God for financial help, thinking He would send money. At times, He has sent money, but more often He has sent me opportunities to earn money by working for it. I had to bear my share of the load.

When we ask for something do we really believe God will deliver? Do we really believe that mountains will move? If we trust God enough to be able to say yes to these questions *and* be willing to be a part of the answer, then the mountains will, indeed, move. I am again reminded of the story of Joseph. If we had been in Joseph's place might we have prayed for God to get our older brothers off our back? And if we prayed that prayer, could we have trusted that God was answering that prayer and so much more when He sent us into Egypt? And would we have become a trusted and diligent servant even after being falsely accused and put into prison?

PRAYER HEALS

Jesus prayed for the sick and even the dead. Many of our prayers are made in times of illness, our own and others. These prayers may express concern over the stress created by the illness or the circumstances resulting from the illness, but we always pray about the condition itself. And prayer does make a difference. A study done on heart patients at San Francisco General Hospital and reported in the Southern Medical Journal involved asking a group of outsiders to pray for a group of cardiac patients. Even though the patients weren't told that prayers were being said for them, the study found that they recovered faster than an otherwise identical control group. The study was described in the January 6, 1992, *Newsweek*.

How does this happen? I believe two forces are at work when we pray for our own well-being and that of others. First, and this is always available to us, is the release through prayer of natural forces, forces given to us by God, which influence conditions both in and around us. It is widely accepted that our state of mind can and does influence our bodies. We can think ourselves sick and we can think ourselves well. I am among those who believe that we can share this ability with others. It is a gift from God and He expects us to use this power. When we pray, we think. Our thoughts are often intense and focused on the object of our prayer, a condition that releases this God-given ability to influence our own condition and that of others. There are no time or space limitations, and the effects are not dependent on the person being prayed for knowing that this is happening. In the study done in San Francisco the patients did not even know that they were part of a study.

Secondly, prayer brings God directly into the situation about which we are praying.

He has promised us that this will happen, *"So I say to you; Ask and it will be given to you; seek and you will find; knock and the door will be opened to you." (Luke 11:9).*

He is like the good parent; not interfering but always willing and ready to help out when asked. When we do ask God, we must always do so with the understanding that the answer must be on His terms which may not necessarily be the way we would do things. We must realize that when we pray for God's help, we are asking God to take control and that we are willing to accept His will. This is not always easy but it is the way it must be.

Prayer makes us receptive to God's will

God speaks to us in many ways. We hear Him when we read our Bibles and in worship. We hear Him in the beauty and grandeur of nature. We hear Him in the lives and words of others. But He speaks to us most clearly and most personally when we pray.

One of our problems is that when we pray we seem to think that we have to do all of the talking. Actually, God already knows what we have on our hearts and what we are going to say. We don't have to actually say a word. We probably learn to pray mainly from listening to our ministers pray during church services, but we don't have to pray like that. What we must learn to do is *listen*. Listening to God's voice is the forgotten part and forgotten art of prayer. God wants us to open up so He can come in. So long as we are talking, it is hard for Him to break through. Prayer is mostly a prayerful attitude, not what we say. This does not mean we ignore the Lord's Prayer. It simply means that we don't need to recite the words if the meanings found in that prayer are on our hearts. We do need to listen for God's reply.

When we fail to listen, it is a bit like saying what we have to say and just dumping it in God's lap. Maybe He doesn't want it in His lap. Maybe He wants to tell us what we should do rather than our waiting for Him to do it. If we aren't waiting and listening for the answer, nothing will happen. Communication is a two-way street, and we have to keep our end of the channel open.

We started this chapter recognizing that prayer provides us with our most personal and powerful contact with God, and we want to end on the same note. We know that we don't change God with our requests and appeals to Him. But when we pray, we do honor Him by the very act of turning to Him and we make ourselves available to do His bidding. We also open ourselves up to accept His will and His way. We ask for His intervention, and we must accept His answers. It is this giving of ourselves to Him that makes things happen.

Does God answer prayers? Of course He does. But we must pray as He has taught us if we want to enjoy the fulfillment of His promises. Pray in the Spirit following the model he has taught. Seek His will and be ready to respond.

SOME QUESTIONS FOR THOUGHT AND DISCUSSION

1. How do you feel about the author's statement that "...our most intimate and powerful association with Him comes when we meet Him in prayer"?

2. Do you agree that the diversity in the various versions of the Lord's Prayer found in different translations of the Bible adds to our

understanding of this passage or do the differences trouble you?

3. Does praying influence God to do things He would not otherwise do?

4. How has your prayer life affected you? In what ways is your life different as a result of your prayers?

5. How should your prayer life be changed?

Chapter ix

Stewardship

Remember this: Whoever sows sparingly
will also reap sparingly, and whoever sows
generously will also reap generously. Each
man should give what he has decided in
his heart to give, not reluctantly or under
compulsion, for God loves a cheerful giver.
And God is able to make all grace abound to
you, so that in all things at all times, having
all that you need, you will abound in every
good work.

II Corinthians 9:6–8

Through most of my adult life my only concern
regarding stewardship had to do with how much
money I could afford to give to the church. At times,

that added up to zero, and at other times I was relatively generous. It was only after I met the Holy Spirit that I began to see the question of stewardship in a different light.

Stewardship is a difficult subject for us to deal with. Many ministers limit their sermons on this issue to one or two a year, usually given in connection with the annual budget making for the church. Though nominal attention is given to stewardship of time and talent in these sermons, we all recognize that the primary purpose is to raise money for the church. The ministers don't look forward to delivering these sermons, and we don't look forward to hearing them. Both their timing and their purpose call attention to their fund-raising emphasis, and their results appear to be something less than hoped for. It seems that whatever is tried, the outcome remains pretty much the same; twenty percent of the membership of the church gives eighty percent of its support.

This appears to be the consequence of stewardship being viewed in terms of what we are able and willing to give the church from our possessions, time, and income. We give a part of what is ours to God's work in the church.

But seeing stewardship from that point of view is not based on Biblical teaching. A popular radio talk show host, Rush Limbaugh, has another way of expressing it. He refers to his talent as being "on loan from God." Whatever your views may be regarding Limbaugh's political opinions and the

way he expresses them, he is certainly right about
the source of his talents. In at least one regard,
he speaks for all of us. Our goods, our health, our
talents, our incomes; all that we have, are on loan
from God…Not only are they on loan, but He
expects us to use them quite well while we have
them. We are stewards of all the abilities and gifts
that God has placed in our care. This is made very
clear in the Parable of the Talents:

> Again, it will be like a man going on a
> journey, who called his servants and entrusted
> his property to them. To one he gave five
> talents of money, to another two talents,
> and to another one talent, each according
> to his ability. Then he went on his journey.
> The man who had received the five talents
> went at once and put his money to work and
> gained five more. So also, the one with the
> two talents gained two more. But the man
> who had received the one talent went off,
> dug a hole in the ground and hid his master's
> money. After a long time the master of those
> servants returned and settled accounts with
> them. The man who had received the five
> talents brought the other five.
> "Master," he said, "you entrusted me with
> five talents. See, I have gained five more."
> His master replied, 'Well done, good and
> faithful servant! You have been faithful with
> a few things; I will put you in charge of

many things. Come and share your Master's happiness!' The man with the two talents also came. 'Master,' he said, 'you entrusted me with two talents; see, I have gained two more.' His master replied, 'Well done, good and faithful servant! You have been faithful with a few things; I will put you in charge of many things. Come and share your master's happiness!" Then the man who had received the one talent came. 'Master,' he said, 'I knew that you are a hard man, harvesting where you have not sown and gathering where you have not scattered seed. So I was afraid and went out and hid your talent in the ground. See, here is what belongs to you.'

His master replied, "You wicked, lazy servant! So you knew that I harvest where I have not sown and gather where I have not scattered seed? Well then, you should have put my money on deposit with the bankers, so that when I returned I would have received it back with interest. Take the talent from him and give it to the one who has the ten talents. For everyone who has will be given more, and he will have an abundance. Whoever does not have, even what he has will be taken from him. And throw that worthless servant outside, into the darkness, where there will be weeping and gnashing of teeth."

MATTHEW 25:14–30

In the parable, the term talent literally means a monetary unit worth about one thousand dollars. However, the stewardship principle expressed most certainly extends beyond money to include all of the abundance God has provided for us.

To understand Christian stewardship, we must first recognize that all we have in our care comes from God and belongs to God. We are merely the caretakers. In the very beginning He placed Adam and Eve in charge. He gave them dominion over His creation but He did not give the creation itself to them. They were His managers, the stewards of what He had made and of what still belonged to Him. We have inherited that role and as His stewards He expects us to use His creation well, and to return it to Him with increase. Another way of putting it is to say that when we leave this world it should be a better and richer place than it was when we arrived.

One of the things we have to do, and it is our most important task, is to carry out God's work here on earth. We are to first love God, and secondly, love our fellow man. In order to do this, we must use the resources God has provided and made us responsible for.

Since it is God's vineyard that we work, His creation, we must look to Him for guidance in determining how His abundance should be used. We go to Scripture and our prayer life for answers.

The first guideline we have comes from the Old Testament. Here we find five references to the tithe, or ten percent of all we have in our care, being given to God's work in the temples and synagogues. Here are two examples:

> "A tithe of everything from the land, whether grain from the soil or fruit from the trees, belongs to the Lord; it is holy to the Lord."
>
> LEVITICUS 27:30

> "Bring the whole tithe into the storehouse, that there may be food in my house. "Test me in this," says the Lord Almighty, "and see if I will not throw open the floodgates of heaven and pour out so much blessing that you will not have room enough for it."
>
> MALACHI 3:10

The goods given as tithes were used to provide for religious leaders and erect the buildings used for religious purposes. There were also provisions for caring for those unable to help themselves, especially the widows.

The tithing standard was never presented with a qualifier such as, "If you can afford it." Every person was expected to turn ten percent of what he had over to the religious leaders. This tradition has been passed on in spite of the fact that the New Testament never refers to the tithe as a standard of stewardship. In fact, the tithe belongs in the same category as the other laws that religious people attempted to live up to in the belief that doing so would make them righteous and acceptable to God. Paul talks about this kind of enslavement to the law in Romans:

"Therefore no one will be declared righteous in his sight by observing the law; rather, through the law we become conscious of sin." (Romans 3:20)

Let's go back to the source. All things originate with God. He is the Creator, the Maker of everything that is. This includes our abilities, our knowledge, the opportunities for earning that are available to us, and the earnings themselves. If it seems difficult to imagine that all of these things come from God, it may be because our modern world has become so complicated that we have trouble looking back to the origin of things. Try backing away from today's world and imagine life in more primitive times. From that perspective, it would be easier to see that all of the things we depend on to maintain life originate in God's nature. If we needed protection from the elements, we found a cave and occupied it. Today we build our own caves by hiring someone to build them for us and by paying for the materials and labor they use. Our money is really just a medium of exchange for all of these things we feel we need. Money stands for the God-given goods and abilities we use in our daily lives. So we are still getting everything from God. Even though the connection between us and nature is more complex than it used to be, everything eventually still goes back to God. He is still the source of all things.

If God is the source and the owner of all things and we are His stewards, then stewardship does not involve giving our resources to Him. Instead, it involves our use of His resources as He would have us use them. And that puts a whole different slant on things. We aren't giving anything. We are managing those things for which God has made us responsible.

So the real question is not, "How much should I give?" We really have nothing to give. What we must ask is, "How should I manage what I have been given responsibility for?" The answers to this question will fall into three categories:

1. Establishing and maintaining God's church.

2. Caring for those in need.

3. Caring for oneself.

ESTABLISHING AND MAINTAINING GOD'S CHURCH

God uses us individually as His representatives. He also uses us in groups that we refer to as churches. In fact, the importance of the church as the agency through which God works is made very clear throughout the New Testament. Most of the recorded works of the apostles following Christ's resurrection involved the establishment of churches. In the book of Acts, we read over and over again of the efforts made by Paul and the others to get the first churches established.

Today, we continue in this tradition. However, when we refer to the church we are no longer speaking only of the neighborhood church. In this modern age, the church has expanded to include the work of evangelists like Billy Graham, the church on television and radio, and the powerful impact of God's message delivered by way of the printed word. The church is still a basic part of God's work and certainly a large portion of the resources we are responsible for must be directed to this effort. It is primarily through the church that we reach others with God's good news and for this reason we need to see to it that it receives resources which are sufficient to meet this challenge. We can, and must, do our own personal evangelizing, but if we work through the church our efforts will be even more richly rewarded. God arranged things that way.

And, of course, the church plays a major role in sustaining those of us who are already Christians. I know that we often kick ourselves because we tend to "run out of gas" when we are separated from our main source of spiritual nurture, the church. We think we should be able to maintain ourselves, but the fact is, we need to be fed and that feeding most often comes through our churches. Through the church we reach out to others but we also nourish ourselves.

CARING FOR THOSE IN NEED

There seems to be no question that God would be pleased that some of His resources be used by the church. We show our love for Him through worship and through activities that bring others to Him. But there is also a second commandment, which says, "... *Love your neighbor as yourself.*" *(Mark* 12:31*)*

Loving our neighbor means more than having feelings of concern:

> What good is it, my brothers, if a man claims to have faith but has no deeds? Can such faith save him? Suppose a brother or sister is without clothes and daily food. If one of you says to him, "Go, I wish you well; keep warm and well fed," but does nothing about his physical needs, what good is it?
>
> JAMES 2:14–16

We are obliged to see that all God's people share in the abundance that is all around us. We don't know why God made some of us responsible for a great deal and others for so little, but we do know that it is His will that those with much share with those who are in need.

All we need to do is look around in the community in which we live. There are homeless people. There are those with medical needs who have no money or insurance to help them meet these needs.

Do not get bogged down in trying to determine why God allows certain conditions to exist. We simply don't know the answers to those questions. All we can do is accept the reality of things as they are and then do our best to make things better—for everyone.

If we approach these problems prayerfully, God will let us know how He wants us to respond. As we look at the overall task to be done, we can be overwhelmed by just how enormous it is. But if we turn the job over to God and allow ourselves to be His instruments in solving the many problems involved, He will lead us to that portion of the task for which we will be responsible. He will lead us to the task, and He will see to it that we have the skills, knowledge, feelings, and funds needed to accomplish our part of the job. God has the means available to get the job done. What He needs is a group of willing and enthusiastic stewards who will use the means carefully and in accord with His plan. That's where we come in.

CARING FOR OURSELVES

If we are to be God's stewards, we must take care of ourselves. Some of the resources we have at our disposal must be used to keep us in shape to do the jobs God has for us to do. When we are ill, out of work, or impoverished, we can't be effective stewards.

We are responsible for the care and upbringing

of our children. We must feed, clothe, and educate them as we prepare them to take their places in this world. The things we teach them, the love we offer them, and the nourishment we give to our bodies are all part of our stewardship. Perhaps it is through our children that we can best see God's gifts to us multiplying.

We must first be financially, emotionally, and spiritually healthy if we are to help others reach these goals. We must accept the gifts that God offers us which make us healthy, then return them to Him through His church and through helping others.

It should be clear by now that stewardship is not a matter of giving a part of what we own to the church. We can understand why the New Testament does not speak of percentages of giving. It is a matter of using everything that God has given us to carry out His work. We must use the time, the abilities, the money, and the love that He has placed in our care to fulfill His commandments, and we must do it with enthusiasm because we really care. "God loves a cheerful giver" is not an empty phrase. It describes the attitude we must have if we are to be His effective stewards.

If we can experience stewardship in this fashion, as using God's resources to His glory and for His work, and not as a matter of giving a portion of what is ours to God's work, we are prepared to fulfill the New Testament standard of stewardship. We will no longer concern ourselves with questions such as,

"How much should I give?" Instead it will be a matter of how to manage everything in order to be the best steward we can be.

It is a certainty that those who are effective stewards, who are effective channels of God's blessings, will be called on to manage even more. They will have more love, more talents, and maybe even more money put into their care. This will continue for as long as we remain faithful stewards. As soon as we decide that what we are doing is giving away our own resources, and especially if we begin to resent the giving, the blessing we have been receiving will be cut off. The abundance that God has promised, whether it be financial, spiritual, emotional, or physical, or some combination of these, will continue to be ours for as long as we joyfully use that abundance to accomplish God's work. If we cease being a channel and become a reservoir, storing up things for ourselves, the abundance will soon dry up. It's a law.

SOME QUESTIONS FOR
THOUGHT AND DISCUSSION

1. What makes discussion of stewardship so difficult?

2. How do you feel about the author's contention that stewardship has more to do with managing God's resources than it has to do with giving?

3. Why do you think the New Testament writ-

ers avoided giving a definite stewardship standard such as a "tithe"?

4. Should we consider our own needs as part of our stewardship? Is the need to keep ourselves fit for God's service a genuine aspect of stewardship or just a way to avoid putting money in the collection plate?

5. Are our churches putting too many resources into their own programs and buildings and not enough in outreach to others?

CHAPTER X

Being a Christian

*"In the same way, let your light shine before
men, that they may see your good deeds
and praise your Father in heaven."*
MATTHEW 5:16

When we began our search for a deeper walk with
God we recognized that the first step in becoming a
Christian is hearing the Word. If others are to know
about Christ, it is up to those of us who already know
Him to spread the Word. Others cannot know about
Him if someone doesn't communicate the Gospel.

How are we to spread the good news about Christ
to the rest of the world? Isn't this the business of our
preachers and missionaries? It is, indeed, the business of preachers and missionaries to see that the

Gospel is spread to the far ends of the earth. But the task does not fall to them alone. All of us who profess to be Christians are under the same commitment as those who have given their lives over to full-time Christian service. In fact, we are all in full-time Christian service as witnesses. In one way or another we are telling all the world what Christianity is all about and what it means to us, everywhere we go, everyday.

Of course, most of us cannot literally travel around the globe preaching the Gospel. That really wouldn't be feasible, would it? If all of us did that and we succeeded, pretty soon the whole world would be filled with Christians scurrying around looking for someone to tell the Good News. We do need those who are called to go abroad and have the gifts of the Holy Spirit that are needed to fulfill that mission. Most of us are clearly not called to that kind of service. But that doesn't relieve us of the responsibility to witness where we are with the gifts we have. There is a song about peace that contains the line admonishing us to recognize that world peace must begin with each of us. It must begin with individuals. And so it is with the spread of the Gospel. It must begin with each of us, at home, at work, where we live.

This puts the burden squarely on our shoulders. It is our job and if we truly believe what we profess to believe, our witness will be clearly evident to those around us. But I can hear some of you saying, "I know all of that. But how about telling me how to do it. How do I express my faith to those around me?"

There are a number of ways to witness and we will look at some of them shortly. But first, we must be sure of what we believe. If our own Christianity is shallow, if we are not sure ourselves that we truly believe, our witness will be ineffective. It may very well have a negative effect. If my Christianity is merely superficial, a façade I carry around with me, and does not include a deeply held belief in a personal, caring God, the need for salvation, an assurance that we are saved through the grace of God made possible through the life, death, and resurrection of Jesus Christ, and that God not only saves us for eternity but also goes with us each day we are here on this earth, my witness is hollow and meaningless. Hypocritical witness is worse than no witness at all.

Witnessing can take a number of forms:

1. Full-time ministry

2. Talking with others on a personal level

3. Teaching

4. Artistic talents

5. Our behavior

6. Let's look a bit more closely at each
   of these.

MINISTRY

Perhaps you feel that you would like to be in what we call full-time Christian service, but think you don't have what it takes to do the job. Be assured that if you are called by God, the gifts you need will be given to you. Those who are truly called by God are blessed with all the talents they need to glorify Him in the tasks to which He has called them.

Some preach. Those who are truly called and gifted preach with a power that is evident to all who hear them. It is a power that takes their preaching far beyond the making of a good speech. But the power is not in the words they use. Many of us could say the same words in a manner that conforms to the requirements of a good speech. But those preachers who are gifted by the Holy Spirit preach with an authority that can come only from God. It is a power that takes their preaching far beyond the making of a good speech and into the realm of prophecy. It goes beyond words and into God's true message which can be given only by those gifted to do so.

Those who preach with this power can be found in all kinds of settings. We have all heard them. Some are in small, local churches and some speak to world-wide audiences. Each is called to witness in the special way and in the special place in which God needs them. Their witness, through their preaching, is a tremendous force for God.

We must all remember that being gifted places a special responsibility on us. It seems very clear that if God gives us a gift, He expects us to use it, and to use it in a way that glorifies Him. Gifts are not to be squandered, wasted, or used in ways that do disservice to God. At the very least, we must give God the credit for whatever gifts we may have and if called to a special kind of service, answer the call with the assurance that everything we need will be provided and give God the glory.

TALKING WITH OTHERS

For most of us the most frequent opportunity to witness will come in interactions with those people we are with each day; family, friends, and co-workers. This is the kind of personal witness that I had hoped for during those many years in which I struggled with my own beliefs. I felt that there must be someone among the people with whom I came into contact on a regular basis for whom Christianity was a real and meaningful force. But no one ever came forward to speak to me on a personal level about their faith.

Until quite recently this lack of personal communication troubled me. I began to question whether anyone outside of the clergy did truly believe.

Then it dawned on me. I had never asked. I had

never let anyone know that I needed to talk about the spiritual dimension of my life. I kept quiet for reasons I cannot explain.

I can hear some of you saying that someone should have come forth and spoken to me without waiting for me to ask, and I can appreciate that viewpoint. I often criticize myself for not being more forceful in approaching others. But there is another side to this issue.

How do you react to being approached by someone who was not invited? I can tell you that if a person hammers me with their opinions without listening to mine or is unwilling to discuss issues about which I have questions, I would turn him away. Not only that, I might very well develop a negative attitude toward the message as well as the messenger. My feelings are rather strong about this. I believe that the "door-to-door, collar everyone you meet" approach will result in alienating many people, pushing them even further away and reducing the likelihood that they will seek the Gospel message with an open heart.

For most of us the most effective witnessing to our friends and families will come when they turn to us because they sense that we have something they need. Deep within they are feeling the yearnings of that spirit that makes us God's children. They know that they need to reach out to God, but they need a helping hand to find the way. Ours can, and should be, that helping hand. This is when our talks, our witness, will be most likely to bear fruit. When others want and need what we have, they will listen and take heed to our message.

We must trust God in this. When someone has reached that point at which he or she needs the witness, the helping hand, we can be assured that God will provide that for them. And we can be assured that when the circumstances are right, God will give us the words, skills, and feelings we must have to meet the seeker's needs. We, as Christians, must be willing to serve in this capacity with the assurance that God will be with us all the way. It is a privilege, an honor, and a responsibility as Christians for us to glorify God in that way.

Some of us may be called upon often to witness in this personal way. Others of us may seldom or never be called. What we all must do is "walk the walk" and be prepared to answer yes when we are called on for this service.

TEACHING

The Word of God, including the Gospel message, is often spread through teaching. By teaching, I mean a planned and purposeful presentation of God's Word to others. This may be in a Sunday school, courses in school, or in planned Bible studies. Some of us may also provide systematic Bible study to our families at home.

In our country, the United States of America,

almost everyone is exposed to some instruction based on the Bible. Many children attend Sunday school or Vacation Bible School at the church their families attend. Some adults also attend Sunday school and Bible study groups sponsored by their church. Though there is a great deal of controversy in our public elementary and high schools regarding all kinds of instruction and activity of a religious nature, many youngsters attend private or home schooling where instruction based on Scripture is given. Many colleges, both public and private, offer Bible courses. Most of us have had some Biblical instruction at some point in our lives.

Those educators who make the decisions to offer Bible study and those who teach these courses are witnessing. They are witnessing to the importance of such study, and they are witnessing on a very personal level by giving their time and talents to this work. Many people, in their personal testimonies, include the influence of some teacher whose efforts inspired them and others in their studies and in their Christian walk.

When the opportunity to teach is presented, many of us say no. We claim that we are not expert enough, or we don't know how to teach, or we don't have the time. We find some excuse to avoid taking on the responsibility. But if it is God who is calling us to this kind of witness, He will, as in all other things, give us the gifts we need to meet the challenge. If God calls and we turn Him down, we are showing a lack of trust in Him to give us what we need to handle the job He has given us. And that unwillingness to do the job and that lack of trust becomes our witness. If those of us who profess to be believers cannot trust God to show us the way, how can we expect others who might be watching us, to obey and follow Him?

ARTISTIC TALENTS

The Christian's life is dedicated to the glory of God. Praising God, lifting Him up, is what life is all about. This is true for all of us. But God has given some people special artistic gifts. These special gifts may include painting, crafting, music, writing, drama, or any other artistic talent. The person who is gifted in any way is responsible for using that talent to express God's glory to the world.

Through the contributions of these gifted people, we come closer to God in two ways. First, in the direct revelation of God that comes to us through the music, art, or writings that tell us how God has touched the life of the artist. We may read how God has blessed the life of the writer or someone known by the writer. We may hear how God has touched the life of the musician. When a truly gifted gospel singer sings of God's love, we are better able to understand what God's love is like. We learn about God from the witness of those who are especially gifted in expressing how God has affected their lives.

The second, and less direct but often just as pow-

erful witness, comes when the artist recognizes that
God is the source of the artistic gift. All gifted singers do not sing gospel music, but all of them received
their gift from God whether they realize it or not.
When they acknowledge this publicly, they are glo-
rifying God and they are reminding us all to recognize that our blessings come from Him.

When we return to God the gifts He has given
us by living in a way that exalts Him, we are witnessing in the fullest sense of the word. As I write
these words I am deeply aware of this responsibility.
If, by sharing what God has meant to me, I can help
you draw closer to Him, I believe I have glorified
Him and been of help to you. That is my task. I
must not hide my light, but I must allow it to shine
for all to see.

Our Behavior

Read the following excerpt from a nationally syndi-
cated newspaper column written by Cal Thomas:

> America has moved through what theologians
> have called post-Christian age into an anti-
> Christian period in which the old self-
> evident truths are no longer self-evident, at
> least not to a majority of citizens. A minority
> of traditional Christians now appeal to the
> definers of culture and government officials
> to reflect these values, ideas and beliefs that

the United State either once accepted or, at least, did not oppose. But cultural change has passed these Christians by, largely because of their failure to confront those in control and because they have lost a moral power from too much fraternization with the kingdom of this world For Christians to gain the respect, if not always the approval, of those who define culture, they must first get their own house in order. Surveys have shown that Christians are divorcing at the same rate as non-Christians. So much for "family values." People who say they are Christians are getting abortions at a rate as high or higher than those who profess a different faith or no faith at all. Too many preachers tolerate 'sin in the camp because they are more interested in building big congregations and church construction projects and their next pastoral assignment than they are in preaching the uncompromising and uncomfortable message contained in the Gospel.

I don't want to believe what this columnist is saying. The notion that being a Christian has no significant influence on our behavior is very difficult for me to accept. And, of course, the writer's observation may not be entirely accurate. However, its accuracy is not really the point. The point is that from what he has seen of Christians and the studies he has read, he can see no difference between the behavior of those who claim to be Christians and everyone else. How is that for a witness? No matter what we say, no matter how many books we write or songs we sing, it all goes for little or nothing if we do not demonstrate in our behavior that being a Christian makes a difference in the way we live. Are you going to listen to and heed the "witnessing" of someone who is arrogant, deceitful, and unwilling to share with needy others? Of course, you won't. Their pious spoken words are betrayed by their actions. Their true witness is in their behavior, not in what they say.

When others see the changes that come about in us through the power of the Holy Spirit and realize that we have something that makes us different, that is our most effective witness. When we can love those who are not lovable, when we can give when others take, when we can weather the storms and tragedies of life with calm assurance, giving God all the praise and glory, and when, even in our sin, we hear and respond to God's voice calling us back, that is our witness. Others see these qualities and respond. We need not twist their arms. We need only to show in the way we act what God's love is all about.

Minister to others, speak to those who would hear, pray for those who won't. Teach and use your talents to glorify God, but most of all, do these and all things in love, love of God and love of our neighbors.

Jesus made it very clear that love is the key to our Christian life when He said:

> …Love the Lord your God with all your heart and with all your soul and with all your mind. This is the first and greatest commandment. And the second is like it: Love your neighbor as yourself. All the Law and the Prophets hang on these two commandments.
>
> MATTHEW 22:37–40

And Paul also spoke eloquently of the importance of love in that great thirteenth chapter of I Corinthians which concludes with this familiar verse, *"And now these three remain: faith, hope and love. But the greatest of these is love." (I Corinthians 13:13)*

We must recognize that there are those whose hearts are hardened and whose backs are turned to God. We must not be defeated when we seem to fail to reach these souls. We can never know when a seed we have planted will take root. We know that some ground is rocky and barren, but we continue to love and give God the task of reworking that soil.

SOME QUESTIONS FOR THOUGHT AND DISCUSSION

1. How do you define witnessing?

2. How do you witness? Do you know others who witness in different ways?

3. Describe some situations in which you failed to witness as effectively as you might have.

4. How have others effectively witnessed to you?

5. How do you feel about the author's belief that our efforts to witness are ineffective if we don't demonstrate the fruit of the Spirit in our own lives?

Epilogue

I dedicated this book to my wife, Nancy, because she led me to a saving encounter with Jesus Christ and for her help in preparing this manuscript. But I also dedicate it to God, Himself, for healing my body when I had such a devastating heart attack, and after that inspiring me to continue this work. He gets the praise and the glory for any good results that have come from this effort to seek a deeper walk with Him. If this book has led you to examine more closely your own walk, I am sure God is pleased, I am pleased, and I am honored to have been able to help you along your way. God bless you always.

H. STUART SMITH